ADOLPHUS F. MONROE.

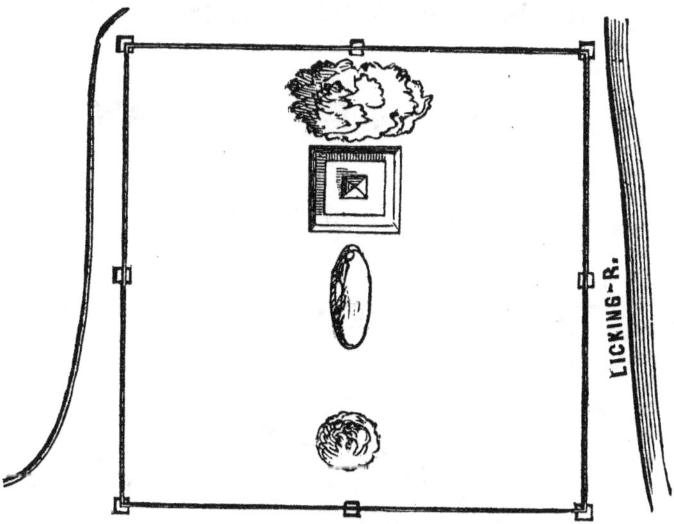

"When I am gone, take me to Kentucky—take me from here, and bury me upon one of the islands above Falmouth, 'St. Helena,' or 'Lovers' Retreat.' Inclose it as I have directed; plant a weeping-willow at my head, and a cedar at my feet."

THE

LIFE AND WRITINGS

OF

ADOLPHUS F. MONROE,

WHO WAS

HUNG BY A BLOOD-THIRSTY MOB

IN

CHARLESTON, ILL.,

ON THE

15TH DAY OF FEBRUARY, 1856,

FOR KILLING HIS FATHER-IN-LAW,

NATHAN ELLINGTON, ESQ.,

In Self-Defense.

CINCINNATI:
PRINTED FOR THE PUBLISHER.
1857.

THE

LIFE AND WRITINGS

OF

ADOLPHUS F. MONROE.

ADOLPHUS FERDINAND MONROE, the subject of this memoir, was born in the town of Falmouth, the county-seat of Pendleton County, Kentucky, on the 6th day of November, 1827. His parents were Jeremiah and Maria Monroe, who, though in very moderate circumstances, always maintained a position of high respectability. The former dying, at a very early period in the life of the son, whose history we are about very briefly to narrate, he was left in the care of that mother for whom his affection seems never to have been diminished, and upon whose prayers alone he might lean in the absence of the temporal advantages of wealth and position. She was not unworthy the trust which devolved upon her, and, with the unselfish affection and high resolve of a woman's nature, discharged it with fidelity.

Falmouth is a beautiful village situated at the confluence of Main and South Licking Rivers, and surrounded by scenery which it would delight the poet to describe or the painter to sketch. It has its history too; and the more ancient of the village gossips delight, of winter evenings, by the roaring fireside, to recount, to their more youthful auditors, the stories of Indian depredations in the neighborhood, and of attacks upon the town itself by a joint force of British and savage warriors, when on their way to the interior of Kentucky, to expel the white man forever from the soil of "The Dark and Bloody Ground."

Amid scenes and under influences like these, it is not remarkable that young Monroe very early manifested a precocity of intellect and a quick, ardent and susceptible temperament. Intelligent, gay and sprightly, he became the idol of his mother in her bereavement, and aware that he must look alone to his intellectual superiority for position in society, she left nothing within her power untried to give him the advantages of a good education. He was sent to the village school—not one of the highest order, but the best, that she could command—and in that way obtained sufficient elementary knowledge to enable him when he attained a suitable age to begin the world as a schoolmaster, in which useful and peaceful occupation he continued until his removal to Charleston, Illinois, in the month of February, 1852.

His mind was of a highly poetic cast. He was subject to great and rapid changes of feeling;—one moment as gay as the bird whose morning song filled his soul with pleasure; the next, perhaps, in tears, and with a heart full of sorrow;—now, merry and cheerful, and anon torn and convulsed by a tempest of passion. But, like the summer cloud which discharges its solitary thunderbolt and then dissolves in sunshine, so with him, the paroxysm was soon over and gave way to love and smiles. In fact, his was one of those natures whose very imperfections we fall in love with, because we feel that they are the excesses which are wont to spring from warm and generous hearts.

He was devoted to the sex, and with his characteristics it would be singular indeed had he been less popular than he was with the gentler half of humanity. In appearance he was highly prepossessing. About five feet eleven inches in height, slender and delicate, with acomplexion fair to effeminacy, flaxen hair, unfathomable blue eyes, a forehead broad, high and intellectual, with an air of easy self-possession; brave and generous, high spirited and wayward, intelligent and handsome, he was the very impersonation of all that is captivating to woman.

Among his literary remains, are to be found many evidences of a high poetic talent. Thrown off on the spur of the occasion, rapidly written and never pruned, never receiving the benefit of that careful revision which authors, jealous of their fame, bestow upon their productions, they, yet, abundantly display the fact that the writer of them was no ordinary man.

While the tender passion seems to have been the leading theme which has employed his mind and heart, we find that he has not wholly forgotten, in the transports of youth and youthful passion, to devote a page to the praises of his mother, nor neglected the claims of early friendship. The wild and romantic scenery of his native village has not been omitted, and he dwells with fond and faithful devotion upon the spots hallowed by the recollections of his early life. The school-house where he first received the rudiments of his education; the willow-covered island to which he appears to have often retired to muse and be alone, and the river, as it went roaring or murmuring by, seems to be as clear in his mind and as dear to his heart when he writes of them as if they were present to his sight.

Upon his removal to Charleston, he was engaged as a clerk in a drugstore, and continued in that employment up to the date of his marriage, without the occurrence of any incident at all material to this memoir. Of a social turn, with ready wit, good address, with excellent conversational power, and with much proficiency as a mimic, his society was much sought after and enjoyed by the young men of the place. His career may have been somewhat varied at this time by some of those frolicksome irregularities of which young men, thoughtlessly, rather than from any bad design, are sometimes guilty, but they passed off and were soon forgotten.

In spring of 1853, Monroe became acquainted with Miss Nannie Ellington, daughter of Nathan Ellington, Esq., with whose destiny, from the moment they met, his own seems to have been indissolubly woven. With them the beginning of acquaintance was the commencement of love, and the lapse of a few months found them betrothed and applying to the lady's parents for permission to celebrate the marriage rite. This permission was for sometime denied, but eventually reluctantly given, and the marriage occurred on the 12th of December, 1853.

Notwithstanding the hesitancy which characterized the conduct of Mr. and Mrs. Ellington with regard to this affair, and the well-understood hostility of some of the young lady's friends, hostility founded upon such reasons as almost always break into ripples the course of true love, we find him setting out hopefully on the journey of life with his loved and lovely bride, intoxicated by the happiness of his new situation and dreamless of the disturbed and angry future which awaited him. Doubtless his ardent and buoyant nature led him to picture his coming life as a long vista of happiness through which he was to walk hand in hand with her whom he had chosen as the wife of his young heart. Her subsequent bearing to her husband in the midst of the flaming ordeal through which he was destined to pass, proves that she was a woman in every way calculated to inspire him with the fondest affection and the highest hopes.

But we must leave a scene like this and prepare ourselves for the contemplation of things of a darker hue.

Though wedded to her whom alone he had loved, and though sure of the affection of her young heart, with his marriage began the dark chapter of woe and unhappiness which ended in the death of Monroe. Unfortunately the prejudices which existed against him before the marriage were not softened by that event, and those upon whom it should have had a different effect, seized upon it as the very instrument of their dislike.

The following letter from Monroe to his wife's father, though written with an unsparing pen, will serve to exhibit to the reader's mind the situation in which he was placed and the grievances to which he was subjected. We give it without comment or alteration:

"CHARLESTON, *May* 3, 1855.

"NATHAN ELLINGTON, ESQ.:

"*Dear Sir*—When I called upon you, a few days since, I did it with the best and kindest feelings—I spoke to you as I would to my own father, if he had been living.

"I studiously refrained from saying any thing that might wound your feelings; not telling you half what I had heard, from different sources, much less what your wife had said to *my own* mother, in my own house; nor, what my wife, through the mistaken influence of *her* mother, had been led to say about me and *my* mother. Suppose we calmly look through this matter and analyze it, and see *who* is wrong. I will state all the facts in the case to the best of my knowledge and recollection.

"In the first place, many months ago, I heard from divers persons, that your wife said *you* would never give me any thing;

that I was a *drunkard* and a *gambler;* that I had made a gambler of *Jim;* that I was too lazy to support my family; *and that we would starve if she did not send us something to eat.*

"Well, under these circumstances, I *requested* Nannie to ask her mother not to send any thing more to my house, and to tell her, also, that it was not because I had any thing against any of you, but that I wished to stop the town-tattle. My request made no change. Still I heard the remarks, until, goaded beyond endurance, I threw the butter she sent us in the street. This seemed *harsh*, yet I would do it again, under the same circumstances, and I believe that any and every man, who has a spark of soul or honor in him, would do the same.

"The next day, your wife came to *my* house and boasted to *my mother* that she had never liked the *Monroe family*, and that she had advised Nannie not to marry me, for the Monroes were all a proud and overbearing set, and mistreated their wives; that I was *mad* because you did not give me a farm, etc., all of which, for the first time, my mother told me. Your wife also said that Nannie wanted to leave me, that she should leave me, etc.

"On Sunday, my wife, without ever telling me, locked up the house and went to your house. I came home to dinner but could not get in. When I went home again in the evening, is it so *strange* that I asked her why she did not *stay* as her mother said she should do; that you, and all your family, wanted her to leave me, and that if *she* wanted to go, I was willing? This, under the same circumstances, I will do again, confident that the world will justify me, and conscious that I would be doing no more than my duty before God. Then, for the first time, under intense excitement, I spoke harshly of your wife. Was not the provocation greater than the offense? I think so. I did wrong, 'tis true, to speak harshly of *any* woman, under *any* circumstances; but, who is perfect?

"Yesterday your wife came again to my house, with the open and avowed intention of taking Nannie home; begging her to leave me; telling her that you would support her; that I would soon spend all I had for *whisky;* that she would lead a miserable life with me; that she had better leave me now, while she had but one child; that by the time we had three or four, I would be a dead drunkard; that she had been told, from good authority, that I had been seen drinking at all the crossings and at other places; and, *then*, in my presence, she again acknowledged that she had told my mother that I was mad because you did not give me a farm, together with many other things that she had said, with the simple explanation that *she had heard so*. Then she threw it up to *me* that it was the *fact;* that she had always known that I had married Nannie for her money, and that the only reason she and you had held back from giving me any thing was, that I was a stranger, and you wanted to try me; that now, since you had found me to be a savage, a beast, a drunkard, a gambler, a spendthrift, etc., you would never give me any thing; but, if Nannie would leave me, you would support her and the child.

"Now, sir, after all this, don't you suppose that I had rather *starve* than receive a *cent from you?* Do you think I will suffer my wife ever to receive a cent from *you* or *yours*, while she is my wife? I would sooner starve myself, and see her and my child starve, than do so. If you don't think so, *I do*.

"Again, your wife said that you thought it very foolish, silly, ridiculous and childish in me to believe such things when I heard them. Very '*childish*,' even when it comes to me *directly* from your wife. Yet, you and she, it seems, have a perfect right to believe any thing *you* hear, as law and gospel. But, I suppose, I am not to believe any thing your wife says? If so, well and good. She told me that you threatened, if ever I spoke to you, or gave you any of my 'jaw,' that I would never know what hurt me. Sir, I presume not, from the fact that I think you will never hurt me. Suffer me to suggest to you, that none of *my* name ever knew what it was to fear *another* man; and if you wish to have 'a talk' with me, come peaceably and kindly, as I did to you; come to me as a man, and so you will be met. Rest assured, that, in whatever spirit you come, I will meet you just in the same. If you have 'a talk' for me, very well; come on, say your say, and do your do.

"I am poor, but not so poor as I was when I married your daughter, notwithstanding I am such a spendthrift, that if you gave me any thing, 'I would soon run through with it.' Yes, I plead guilty; I am poor, and so I will be forever, unless I can make a living myself—rest assured of that. *Remember*, I tell you *now*, I, nor my wife, while she is a wife of mine, nor a child of mine, shall ever cost you a dime.' Your wife complained that I never told *you* that I would build in the pasture.' Did you expect me to come to you? I am charged with being a *beast* and a *savage*, and that I mistreat my wife. Nannie, herself, does not, can not, nor will not say I ever spoke an unkind word to her. She never wanted any thing but what I bought; never asked a favor but 't was granted. The only and greatest fault I ever found with her, if you call it so, was, that she did too much work. I did not want her to wash and scrub. I wanted to get help, but she never would have any. My *crime* is, after all, the town-talk and tattle. After your wife threw it up to me that I was mad because you did not give me a farm, etc., then I refused to let you give me *any thing*. *That* is my crime.

"Next, after your wife threatened to take Nannie home, begged her to go, and said that *she* wanted to go, I told her, if she wanted to leave me to do so—that I was perfectly willing. Do you suppose that I would want her to stay with me against her will? No.

"But a few more words and I am done. In the language of old Zack Taylor, 'I ask no favors and shrink from no responsibilities.' Let it be written on my tomb, that I never received a cent from my father-in-law. Never say again that I covet your gold. Remember, this is my last resolve, *here I will live and die, independent of you and yours.*

"The world may judge between us, the rest is between us and our God! A. F. MONROE."

The reader will readily perceive, from the tone of the foregoing letter, the exasperated and goaded condition of the mind of its author at the time it was written. This unhappy family rupture, "the Iliad of all his woes," and the fruitful fountain of all his troubles seems to have wholly absorbed the mind of Monroe. Devoted to his wife, and looking forward from the inauspicious beginning of their union with the most hopeful reliance, that family difficulties would soon be settled, and unjust prejudices soon eradicated; that this union would be the source of all the happiness which springs from conjugal life, what wonder is it that finding the prospect overcast and promised joys suddenly dashed from his very lips, he should express himself as he does in the letter to Mr. Ellington? His own house invaded—his mother—the widow, amid the folds of whose sable garments he had nestled in the hour of her bereavement, and who had spent the energies of her life for him, insulted at his own fireside—his ears assailed every hour by the taunt, that in his apparent regard for his wife there was no touch of unselfish affection, and that it arose from a desire to possess her money—denounced as a drunkard and a spendthrift, the subject of every abusive and opprobrious epithet that would stir the blood to madness, it is scarcely a matter of surprise that he should have written this letter, and concluded it with the wild oath never to receive, or allow his wife or child to receive, the smallest pecuniary favor at the hands of his wife's father. Had the hope of gain been the incentive to his marriage, never did man display so utterly the want of policy, so complete an ignorance of that "fawning which is followed by thrift" Passionate, proud and self-relying, he depended upon no arm but his own for a livelihood, and after the grievances he mentions, it would have required much hardship and many privations to have brought him to the acceptance of favors which he would have regarded as the badges of his shame.

Had he been the possessor of that practical worldly wisdom where ends always justify the means by which they are accomplished, we should have found him in the pursuit of a wholly different line of policy. He would have been humble, meek and submissive, cultivating the art of flattery, echoing loudly the sentiments of others from whom he expected advantages, regardless of their worth, and, finally, worming himself into the confidence and affections of those from whom he expected profit.

Mr. Ellington, at the beginning of this sad chapter of human weakness, which was to be concluded by the tragedy of his own death, was the friend of Monroe. Slowly, however, by the machinations of others, his negative friendship was turned to positive dislike, and, in the end, it was his own violent conduct, prompted, doubtless, by his unkind feeling for Monroe, that lead to his death. Alienated in feeling, with hard thoughts and unhappy suspicion on each side, though no one dreamt of a tragedy, such as was about to be enacted, it required but the happening of some trivial event to hasten the crisis which was impending. That event happened and the crisis came.

On the night of the 18th of October, 1855, James Ellington, the brother-in-law of Monroe, and Byrd Monroe, his cousin, had an altercation in the store of the latter, about an account or note. Monroe's name was mentioned in the course of the dispute, and he, being sent for, came to the store, but took no part in the affair which expended itself in words.

On the morning of the 19th, Monroe was in Norfolk's drugstore giving an account of the difficulty of the previous evening. He was mimicking Byrd Monroe's voice and gestures, and acting the affair over again in his inimitable style. He wound up his story with the remark that the matter would be settled that morning.

At an earlier hour than usual he left the drugstore and started toward his boarding-house. Mr. Moore, the gentleman at whose house he and his wife were boarding, happened to be absent that day, and Monroe started to the house earlier than usual, to ascertain if Mrs. Moore had a sufficiency of wood cut, he having previously sent a boy to prepare as much as she might need. When he set off he took a straight course from the store to the house, which would lead him across the public square of the town. In the street he met Mr. Ellington who appeared to be much out of humor. Inferring from the look with which Mr. Ellington met him that he was angry with him, and apprehending that young Ellington had given him an account of the occurrence of the previous evening, calculated to do him injustice, he desired to know what had been said, and, for that purpose, he said to Mr. Ellington:

"I suppose Jim told you of his *fuss* last night? I was sent for and hunted up but did not see that I had any thing to do with it; so, I only laughed at them." At this Ellington elevated his cane, as if he intended to strike, saying at the same time:

"Yes, you *had* something to do with it; you puppy! Byrd Monroe has been lying for some time, and you denied things you have said to him."

Monroe, stepping back several paces, exclaimed, "Don't strike me with your cane! Byrd Monroe won't say so!"

"He will!" replied Ellington.

"He will *not!*" persisted Monroe.

Mr. Ellington then requested Monroe to go with him to Byrd Monroe's store. Monroe, at first, hesitated, but being urged by Ellington who called to him to "come on," "come along," he went with him.

Arriving at the store they found that Byrd Monroe was absent. Monroe then remarked to Mr. Ellington: "I do not see why you should blame me for every lie that you hear. If, as you say, Byrd and John Monroe have lied, it is no business of mine, but is a matter between you and them. I don't know any thing about this scrape, care nothing about it, nor do I want to know any thing about it—and I don't know why in the devil I am dragged into it."

"I have no doubt in the world that you have told forty lies about it," was the insulting reply of Ellington.

"If I have told *forty*," said Monroe excited, "you have told *sixty!*"

"You trifling puppy! do you talk to me in that way?" exclaimed Ellington throwing out both arms and running at Monroe, who retired several steps as Ellington approached.

The positions of the parties during the conversation and at the commencement of the difficulty were about these: The store-room fronted on the south side of the street running back north. Ellington was standing with his back against the counter running along the east side of the room, with his elbow resting upon the show-case, holding his cane in one hand grasped at the middle. Monroe was standing near a short counter on the west side of the room, and perhaps ten or twelve feet distant from Ellington.

When Mr. Ellington advanced with his right hand he grasped the collar of Monroe's coat, and with his left seized him by the throat, his cane striking Monroe a smart blow upon the forehead and breaking the skin upon his left hand as he threw it up to parry the attack of his assailant. Ellington who was a much larger and stronger man than Monroe, choked the latter back upon the counter. At this time Monroe was completely at the

mercy of his antagonist whose grasp upon his throat was every instant growing tighter, and, as his only resource, since none of the spectators attempted to interfere and separate them, he drew a small pocket pistol and fired, the ball striking Ellington upon the forehead and glancing off, doing him but slight injury.

Ellington then threw Monroe upon the floor, and springing upon him began to beat, gouge and choke him in the most furious style. Monroe could easily have shot him again, but, as he declared, the thought of his wife and child, and that his assailant was the father of that wife, compelled him to forbear. Desirous that no further harm should be done, he called to the spectators to take Ellington away. The only response to his call was made by a man named *Eastin*, who cried out to Ellington: "Stamp him to death! stamp his d—d guts out!" Still no one interfered to stop the difficulty.

At this time, Mr. Dumas J. Van Deren, hearing the report of the pistol that had been fired, ran into the store. According to his statement, Monroe was "*wheezing*" like a man who is choking to death. Van Deren immediately took hold of Ellington, calling out to the bystanders: "Let's part them! For God's sake, gentlemen, don't let them kill each other!" He endeavored to pull Ellington off, who looked up to him and said: "Let me kill him! he has shot me!"

Monroe, by a great effort raised to his knee and fired the second pistol, the ball taking effect in Ellington's heart. At the report of the second pistol, Ellington yielded to Van Deren, who walked with him to his office. Monroe made no attempt to escape, declared he was ready to stand his trial, and was immediately arrested and placed in prison. Ellington lingered until the 28th, nine days after the fatal affray, when he died.

Monroe was brought before an examining court and the result was that he was committed for trial at the ensuing regular term of the Circuit Court for Coles County.

With the death of Ellington began that feeling of violence and lawlessness which finally resulted in the murder of Monroe. For many years the clerk of the Circuit Court, acquainted with almost every man in the county, rich and consequently influential, it is not to be wondered that great excitement prevailed when his death was announced; many and loud were the threats of violence to the prisoner, and it was greatly feared by his immediate friends and by the law-abiding portion of community that his case would be wrested from the properly constituted tribunal, and decided by the mob.

The prisoner, plunged immediately in jail, could not tolerate the prospect of a long and tedious confinement and preferred death itself to his lonely incarceration. Conscious, as he declared himself, of his innocence, and satisfied in his own mind that that innocence would be established could he secure for himself an impartial trial, he determined to insist upon a change of venue in his case, and he asked for a special term of the court to consider his application.

The court was held on Monday, January 14th, 1856. So great was the tumult in the community when it was understood that an application was to be made to have the case tried in another county; so loud the threats of certain violence by the agitators who had resolved that upon such an application being made, they, being well aware that under the circumstances it could not be refused, he should forthwith be hanged, that the prisoner and his counsel were powerless and when the court met, the trial was taken up without any allusion to the proposed motion. Here then we see a man, under the external show of justice, placed at the bar, to pass through the semblance of a fair trial, the issue of which was life or death, surrounded by hundreds, who, with glaring eyes and eager hands, stood around about him already resolved that he should die! What a mockery! What a shameful wicked mockery!

We proceed, however, without further comment to give the proceedings of the court, merely asking the candid and careful attention of the reader to the evidence, and with perfect reliance that he, unawed by a mob and uninfluenced by that stange, wild and ungovernable excitement which pervades all communities at times, can, at the conclusion, but render a verdict of "not guilty!"

THE TRIAL.

On Monday, at 2 o'clock, P. M., the court was called to order, Judge Harlan, presiding. After the selection of a grand jury had been made, and they had received their charge from the bench, the court adjourned.

TUESDAY 15*th*, 10 *o'clock*, *A. M.*

Court was opened. The grand jury returned into court having found the indictment against the prisoner "a true bill."

Court adjourned until 2 o'clock, P. M.

2 *o'clock same day.*—The court was re-organized and a jury empanneled, after which the court adjourned until 10 o'clock next morning.

WEDNESDAY 16*th*, 10 *o'clock*, *A. M.*

The court was opened at the time appointed. The jury was brought down, and the prisoner brought into court and placed at the bar.

A. Kitchell, prosecuting attorney. Capt. William E. Sims and Hon. O. B. Ficklin, appeared for the prosecution. Gen. W. F. Linder, appeared for the defense.

The prosecution proceeded to examine their witnessess. The first one called was

JOHN WILKINSON, who testified as follows:—"I have known the prisoner since last June; knew Mr. Ellington; I arrived here from California on the 14th of last June; was often in Monroe's company; he kept a drugstore in this place; have frequently seen him carry two small Minnie pistols. (Here a pistol was exhibited to the witness.) This is one of the pistols he carried or one just like it.

By the prosecution.—"State if you ever heard Monroe make threats against Nathan Ellington."

Witness.—"I will go back to the time I came here; heard

him, about the second day after my return, speak of the Ellington family; heard him do so almost daily afterward, so that I came to pay very little attention to him; have frequently heard him say that Ellington was an old thief, an old coward, and a d—d old rascal; that Mrs. Ellington was an old prostitute. Have heard him say he would give fifty dollars to any one who would go and tell Ellington what he said about his wife, as he wanted a difficulty with him. One night previous to the difficulty, Monroe had a conversation with me in reference to the Ellington family. I told him Ellington was the last man he should have a difficulty with. He then pulled out two Minnie pistols, and said he had bought them for Jim and the old man, and intended to use them. Heard nothing more, particularly, until the morning of the difficulty. There had been, the evening previous, a difficulty between Byrd Monroe and Jim Ellington. Dolph was in the drugstore that morning, talking about the Ellingtons, as usual, what he would do. I told Monroe this was an old story and all fol-de-rol; he said the matter would be settled that morning. Just then Mr. Ellington came walking out of his office on the foot-logs toward the drugstore. Monroe left the drugstore and met Ellington. Some conversation ensued, and they agreed to go to Byrd Monroe's store. I expected there would be a difficulty and followed after them to see fair play. After they went into the store some conversation passed between them about previous circumstances. Ellington said it was no use to hunt up Byrd and John Monroe, as he had been to them before, and they had always sustained what he said, and denied what Dolph said. Monroe replied, that he had'nt lied, and, if *others* had, he did'nt see why he should be brought into it. George Monroe, then said, 'You must not say they have lied!' Ellington then remarked 'Dolph, you know you have told forty lies upon me and my family.' Monroe replied, 'If I have told forty, you have told sixty.' Ellington, at this, said, 'You must not talk so to me, young man!' putting his hand upon his shoulder. Monroe then stepped back, drew his pistol from his right pocket and fired, the ball giving a flesh wound on the upper part of Ellington's forehead ranging upward and outward. Ellington seized hold of Monroe pushing him against the counter, and partly on it, I think. Then they scuffled down on the floor,

Some one called out: 'Take him off!' Ellington was on the top of Monroe, confining his left hand in which he held the other pistol.

(The witness here described to the jury the position in which the parties were at the beginning of the affray and throughout the struggle, and his relative position to them during the time.)

"Dumas Van Deren ran in at this time, and catching hold of Ellington, partly pulled him off of Monroe and broke his grasp on Monroe's hand, and then the pistol fired. Mr. Ellington then appeared to be enraged and more determined to hurt Monroe, commencing to beat him in earnest. Ellington and Monroe were separated and the latter ran out. I said: 'For God's sake, don't let him escape; he has killed Ellington!' I then went to the bank and found Eastin guarding him."

In reply to a question, witness said he was about twenty feet from them when they met on the street, but, the conversation being carried on in an under tone, he could not hear what they said, except Ellington remarked that they would go over to Byrd Monroe's store. Witness also stated, in reply to a question, that Ellington stated to Monroe that he had previously brought him before Byrd and John Monroe and they had always sustained his (Ellington's) statement. Witness also stated that when Ellington told Monroe he had told forty lies on him and his family, Monroe said, "If I have told forty lies, you have told sixty," stepping back and partly pulling out the pistol in his right pocket, so as to disclose two thirds of it, which he, the witness, then saw. When the pistol was discharged, they were very close together, face to face, Ellington near or against the counter, and Monroe with his hands in his pockets. Monroe stepped back very much excited, and as Ellington put his hand on his shoulder, or took him by the collar, the pistol immediately fired. The pistol was fired as Monroe was against the counter, though he was not on it then. This occurred (witness thinks) on the 19th of October last. Ellington pushed Monroe partly on the counter, his feet hanging off.

(Witness here described to the jury the position of the counter and of the room and the doors of the store.)

"They scuffled from the counter to the floor and were near the middle door. Witness said John Eastin, James Fallen and Geo.

Monroe were there; and that Dumas Van Deren and, perhaps, one or two others, came in after the first pistol was fired. Witness was seven or eight feet from the parties when the second pistol was fired; saw the pistol two or three times in Monroe's left hand while Ellington held it. When the second pistol was fired, Ellington was pretty much on his feet. When Van Deren pulled Ellington partly off they were in front of witness. When Van Deren pulled Ellington it broke his hold on Monroe's hand, and, then, the second pistol was fired. Ellington then began to choke and gouge Monroe, who cried, 'Murder! take him off!' There was no outcry from either of the parties until after the firing of the second pistol. Witness saw Ellington strike no blow previous to the firing of the second pistol."

(Witness here stated that Monroe's pistols were self-cocking and could be discharged by striking on the hammer or pulling the trigger.)

Cross examined:—"The second pistol was fired before Van Deren parted them. Witness was not noticing them all the time, as he sometimes had his eyes on George Monroe. When Ellington had Monroe down Van Deren broke his hold. Didn't see Ellington gouge Monroe before the second pistol was fired. Some twenty seconds, perhaps, intervened between the two fires. After the first pistol was fired, they scuffled on the counter and on the floor. About this time George Monroe came running up with a pistol in his hand; witness pushed him back and told him to let them alone; witness thought he was going to shoot Eastin, and intended to eat him up alive if he did. Ellington was taken off almost immediately after the firing of the second pistol. George Monroe called out to part them and some one said, 'No! let him stamp his d—d guts out!' Witness don't know who made this remark, but thinks it was Eastin.

"Monroe was running on in the drugstore the morning of the difficulty, and witness told him it was an 'old song;' witness had heard so much he was tired of it. About this time, Monroe drank freely and would generally have liquor in him, and when Ellington's name was mentioned he would become excited. Witness frequently heard him say, if Ellington crossed his path he would kill him, and has heard other similar threats. Monroe said, he had been told they were going to tar and feather him, and by G—d, if they came for that purpose, they would meet a warm reception. A great many times when witness had gone into the drugstore, Monroe would be running on about Ellington. Witness would tell him this was an old song; that he had heard it so often he was tired of it, and believed it meant nothing. When Monroe said; 'this difficulty shall be settled this morning,' he was addressing himself perhaps to Hackett, but witness don't know. Monroe said, 'D—n Ellington's old soul, he is afraid to come out and meet me,' and said, in reply to a remark of witness, 'never mind, this difficulty will be settled this morning.' There has been no difficulty between Monroe and witness. Monroe said, in this conversation, that Jim Ellington would brag. Witness replied, that Jim Ellington was a d—d coward, or he would have killed him (Monroe) before now; and that Jim ought not to brag after he (Monroe) left here. In regard to the boys making mention of the Ellington family, to hear Monroe talk about them, witness knows he never did it. When witness saw Ellington in the street he had his cane in his hand; it was a walking-stick of pretty good size; witness did not see Ellington wave his cane as if to strike, nor did witness hear Monroe say, 'Don't strike me with your cane, Mr. Ellington.' In the conversation at Byrd Monroe's store, Monroe said, 'By G-d! if I have told forty lies, you have told sixty!' As well as witness remembers, Monroe's back was against the counter; witness did not see precisely how Ellington held Monroe; when Van Deren took hold, to separate them, Monroe was on the floor, under Ellington, with his face downward. After the second pistol was fired, Ellington took hold of Monroe in earnest, and Monroe began to cry, 'Murder! take him off!' etc. Witness did not see Mr. Cole in the store at this time, and does not remember saying to any one, 'let them alone! another pistol will be fired!'

"In answer to the question why he didn't let George Monroe go up, witness said it was because he saw George had a pistol in his hand, and besides, after seeing Ellington have Monroe by the hand, he knew Monroe couldn't shoot him. Has frequently heard Monroe say he would give fifty dollars for a difficulty. Monroe was in the habit of carrying his hands in his pockets. When the second pistol was fired witness didn't see Monroe use it. Monroe drew the first pistol from his right pocket."

JOHN EASTIN.—"Have known Ellington since 1830, and Monroe for five or six years; have heard Monroe have many talks about Ellington and family for several months before the affray; Monroe would become very much excited on such occasions; would say how the difficulty between them came about and curse the family, sometimes one member of it and sometimes another; would say that Mrs. Ellington was a d—d old bitch; that she led Ellington by the nose and wanted to lead him (Monroe). These conversations were quite common. He said he had made Ellington eat his own words and G—d d—n his old soul if ever he crossed his path he would kill him. Witness had talked to Monroe frequently, and told him he was doing Ellington injustice. He would reply that Mrs. Ellington led her husband by the nose; would curse and threaten Ellington, and say, if such and such things happened, he would kill him. Witness told him that Ellington would not notice his talking around, but, if he went to Ellington and talked in this style, that Ellington would slap him, and then Monroe would kill him and this would be the end of it. Monroe would swear he was prepared and would kill him. Monroe had two pistols; have seen him shooting these pistols in the back part of the drugstore, but heard no threats at such times; saw him shooting three or four times, perhaps oftener. On one occasion, when witness and others were in the second story of the drugstore, Monroe had been telling his troubles, when Ellington came out of his office; seeing him, he took out his pistols, saying, 'You d—d old s–n of a b—h; it would do me good to blow you through!' This occurred two or three weeks before the affray, perhaps longer. Witness frequently heard the prisoner talk of his troubles. He was always excited and said he was badly treated by all the family except Lizzie; thinks he always excepted her; can't name any particular day on which he made threats; it was so common an affair, that the boys would frequently laugh about it, and Dick Norton would sometimes say, 'Hold on, boys; Dolph will soon be in and branch out on the Ellington family.' On the evening previous to the killing, there had been a difficulty between

Jim Ellington and Byrd and Dolph Monroe about something, which led, witness supposes, to this affair. Dolph Monroe and Ellington went over to the court-house and talked the matter over and left in pretty good humor. Next morning witness was in the drugstore, when Dolph came in a good deal excited about the difficulty of the previous evening. Shortly after Monroe quit talking about the matter, Ellington came out of his office and walked across the street toward the drugstore. The prisoner went out and met him about the middle of the street. Witness expected a difficulty and went out to the post on the sidewalk. Monroe spoke to him, but witness did not hear what he said. Ellington seemed to be offended and a little excited; he was walking with his cane, and partly raising it up, he said, 'You puppy, don't talk to me that way!' The prisoner said, 'Byrd Monroe said so,' and Ellington replied, 'Byrd Monroe will not say so.' Witness thought, from the movements of both parties, that Ellington had a notion to strike Monroe. Dolph said, 'Byrd Monroe will say so,' when Ellington replied, 'Let's go to the store, and Byrd will say no such thing.' They then started, Monroe rather reluctantly, witness thought. Witness, expecting a difficulty, followed. Byrd was not in. Ellington said: 'I have been with you to Byrd and John before, and they always sustained my statements.' Monroe replied, that he didn't see why, if others lied, he should be brought into the scrape. They talked on and became more calm. Witness thinks Wilkinson, Fallin and John Monroe, only, were in at the time. Witness stepped out to see a man, and as he got out on the pavement heard short words; turned to go back and heard the first pistol; ran in and saw Ellington have hold of Monroe against the counter. In the scuffle, Ellington threw Monroe near to the back door. George Monroe came running up once or twice with a pistol, and witness pushed him back. Monroe was rather on his hands and knees, and Ellington on him, as witness thought. Dumas Van Deren ran in at this time, saying: 'Don't let the men kill each other!' He grasped Ellington, partly took him off, and, then, rather let him go, at which time the second pistol was fired. Witness did not see the pistol before during the affray, but saw one afterward. Witness caught Monroe and held him until he got to the front door, at which place he let him go. Ellington then said, 'Don't let that man escape!' Witness went out after him and found him at the bank. He seemed to be considerably scratched and bruised. Witness told him to remain until the sheriff came, and the prisoner replied, that he didn't want to escape. The sheriff came and arrested him. The injuries done to Monroe's eyes were, for the most part, done after the second pistol was fired, and witness heard no hallooing from Monroe until after the second fire."

Cross examined:—"Mr. Ellington, in the conversation before the drugstore, proposed to go to Byrd Monroe's; prisoner rather hesitated, when Ellington said, 'come along,' and they, then, went over walking side by side. Monroe would frequently tell over his troubles, sometimes speaking of one thing and sometimes of another; would frequently speak of things somebody had told him. He seemed to think he had been badly treated; said Ellington had refused to pay for a set of china which he had bought for his (Monroe's) wife. He seemed to think it hard that Mrs. Ellington had ordered his mother from his own house. Never heard him say Ellington had threatened to tar and feather him. Have heard him say Ellington was a liar; that he had so and so, and that he (Monroe) had called on him and made him take his words back; that had he not taken them back he would have blown him through. In the scuffle on the floor, Monroe's face was turned toward the floor; Ellington seemed to be gouging him. Monroe did not cry out until the second pistol was fired, after which Ellington seemed anxious to hurt him. The second pistol was fired after Van Deren had partially parted them. The whole affray lasted, probably, a minute. George Monroe ran up and cried, 'Fair play!' Witness said, 'Let them alone, let him stamp his guts out!' Said this after the first fire and before the second. George Monroe came up with a pistol in his hand. I never saw Ellington strike or kick Monroe; thought he was gouging or choking him; never heard Monroe call out for help until after the second pistol was fired. In the conversation between Ellington and Monroe on the street, Ellington raised his cane as if about to strike; I heard the remark, 'You shan't talk to me that way, you puppy.' Monroe had his hands in his pockets, and stepping back, said, 'Byrd Monroe *had* said so and so, and *would* say so.' Ellington replied that

'Byrd Monroe wouldn't say so,' and then said, 'let's go over to Byrd's,' and Monroe seemed to go rather reluctantly. In the threats which Monroe would make, he would say if Ellington disputed his word he would do so and so. Witness would tell him that Ellington wouldn't mind his talking around the streets, but if he went to Ellington and talked that way to him he would slap him over, and Monroe would reply, that if he did he would blow him through. Witness don't know that he ever heard prisoner say that he intended to attack Ellington and kill him. Monroe would generally speak as though he would go and make Ellington acknowledge so and so, and if he didn't he would kill him. Has heard him say all he asked of them was to be let alone, and that if it were not for Mrs. Ellington he could get along. Witness knows of Monroe preparing to move away from here; has advised him to take his wife and go away, and that they would then live happily. He talked as if he intended to go away. Witness don't remember any threats after his making preparations to leave. In these conversations, he would say he intended to protect his mother, and to take her with him wherever he went. Witness told him not to take his mother as that would not satisfy Mrs. Ellington. Monroe said Ellington had lied on him, and he had made him take it back, and that if he had not, taken it back, he would have killed him."

James W. Fallin.—"Was present at the difficulty. Saw Ellington and Monroe talking on the street, near the drugstore, but couldn't hear what they said. They went from the street to Byrd Monroe's drugstore and witness followed. Heard Monroe, at the store, say to Ellington, 'You did say so, or Byrd Monroe lies.' Ellington said, 'You have told forty lies on me and my family,' and Monroe replied, 'If I have told forty, by G—d, you have told sixty!' Ellington then put his hand on Monroe's shoulder and said, 'Young man, you must not talk to me in that way!' and, perhaps, gave him a push. Monroe fired; Ellington then took hold of him; had him on the counter first, and then on the floor. About this time, Dumas Van Deren ran in, and, taking hold of Ellington partly pulled him off. The second pistol was fired. When witness first saw them talk in the street, they were directly west of Ellington's office. Could not hear what they said, except something about going over to Byrd Monroe's store. Witness was then on the door-sill. Monroe said in the store, to Ellington, 'You shouldn't blame me for Byrd's lies,' and then Ellington told him he had told forty lies; to which Monroe replied, 'If I have told forty, by G—d, you have told sixty,' stepping back with both hands in his pockets. At this Ellington laid his hand on him, perhaps giving him a little push, and then the first pistol was fired. Monroe was standing with his back to the counter and Ellington faced him. When the pistol fired, Ellington merely put his hand on his shoulder. Witness could not describe the scuffle, he was so much excited; Ellington was on top; didn't see their hands. Van Deren caught Ellington by the back and pulled him nearly straight up and then the second pistol was fired. After the second pistol was fired, don't remember any more scuffling, didn't see the pistol, don't remember any outcry."

Cross examined:—"Didn't see Monroe when Ellington had him down. Van Deren separated them just after coming in."

At the request of Gen. Linder, John Eastin was recalled.—"Ellington was a large and very stout man; witness once considered himself stout, and Ellington could always handle him. Ellington could handle Monroe very easily; he weighed about two hundred pounds, and his health had never been impaired.

E. S. Norfolk.—"Knew the prisoner; knew he was in the habit of carrying a couple of small Minnie pistols (a small pistol was exhibited to witness, which he said was like Monroe's). Don't know when he got them; knew he had them five or six weeks before the killing. He always kept them loaded, and have seen him shoot at a mark with them in the back room of the drugstore. He shot them frequently, and would always load them. Never heard him make direct threats; have heard him say if ever Ellington brought the hands over to tar and feather him he would hurt them. Monroe said, they had denied so and so, and if they had acknowledged that they had said so and so, he would have hurt them. Never heard any direct threats more than, if Ellington crossed his path, he would hurt him. Have heard Monroe talk this way perhaps every day, and sometimes several times a day. He would always become excited when he talked of the difficulties between him and the Ellingtons."

Cross examined:—"Was with Monroe in the drugstore every day, and never heard him make a direct threat; it was always conditionally. Have heard him say he always intended to act on the defensive, but he would branch off."

The counsel for the prisoner asked the witness if it was not customary for young men about town to carry pistols? To this question objection was made by the attorney for the State, and, the point having been discussed, the court sustained the objection.

R. H. Norfolk.—"Knew that Monroe carried pistols before the encounter with Ellington; he carried them in the pockets of his pantaloons. Thinks he usually had his hands in his pockets; thinks he had the pistols two or three months before the difficulty with Ellington; have heard him say if Ellington ever crossed his path he would hurt him; he did not say he would kill him; have heard him curse him, say he was a d—d low rascal and use other similar epithets. Never heard him say he would shoot or kill him. I once told him that Ellington could whip him, and he replied that he could shoot Ellington before he could get to him; have heard him say he *ached* to get into a difficulty, with him; have heard him say this often; he shot his pistol off frequently, though perhaps not daily. Monroe and witness were partners in the drugstore up to a few weeks before the killing; witness was in the drugstore the morning before Ellington was killed, and Monroe was there firing his pistol; said he was going to get Mr. Ellington, Jim Ellington and Byrd Monroe together, and he would hurt some of them yet. The morning of the difficulty, Monroe said something about some one having lied. Witness saw Monroe and Ellington meet on the street. Monroe said nothing when he went out of the drugstore to meet Ellington. He said, that morning, he would make some of them swallow the lie. Witness didn't think he was in earnest. Didn't hear any thing they said on the street; saw no cane drawn by Ellington; didn't know which of them proposed going to Byrd Monroe's store. Never heard Monroe say he drank to raise his courage."

Cross examined:—"Never heard Monroe make a direct threat."

The witness was asked if he had ever heard Monroe say he only intended to defend himself? He replied: "The prisoner told me one day, 'I intend to defend myself.'"

J. E. WYCHE.—"Some three or four weeks before the killing of Ellington, Monroe commenced a conversation with me on the street in reference to a business transaction between us. It was near Compton & Mount's store. Monroe requested me to go into the shed part of the store where we sat down. The prisoner said: 'Wiche, I am a little drinking to-day, you see; and I am so on purpose; I want a difficulty with Mr. Ellington; the Ellingtons have called me a coward, and I intend to show them I am not afraid of them.' Witness then told the prisoner nobody thought him a coward, but, if it would gratify him, he might tell Ellington he was not afraid of him, and there drop it; that Ellington was the last man on earth he should kill; and represented to him the unpleasant position in which it would place his wife, she being Ellington's daughter. To all this prisoner seemed to assent. Witness told him as he had now sold out, he had better leave Charleston, as he thought they could not live pleasantly there. Monroe said he intended to leave, but, before he went, he was going to show Ellington that he was no coward. Prisoner said there was no difficulty between himself and his wife, and seemed to censure Mrs. Ellington more than any one else; said that Mrs. Ellington forbade his own mother to come to his house; said he should always defend his mother, she had been such a good friend to him; and that he could not desert her to please anybody. Monroe went on to enumerate various grievances, but he did not say he intended to attack or kill Ellington. Said he wanted a difficulty with him; that the Ellingtons had said he was a coward, and he intended to show them that he was not. Mr. Monroe seemed a good deal moved during the conversation, and, before its close, shed tears freely."

Cross examined:—"Never heard Monroe say he intended to attack or kill Ellington. This conversation occurred three or four weeks before the killing of Ellington, and witness never, on any other occasion, heard Mr. Monroe say any thing about Mr. Ellington or his family."

Court adjourned to 10 o'clock, next day.

Thursday 17*th*, 10 *o'clock*, *A. M.*

Court met and proceeded with the evidence for the prosecution.

Stanley B. Walker.—"Was not present at the difficulty; don't remember any direct threats; has heard Monroe say he would do so and so, under certain circumstances; heard him say so once at the store, Bledsoe and others being present; can't state word for word what he said; he was talking about the Ellington family, for good reasons, as he thought; he said that Mrs. Ellington was a long tongued old b—h, and that probably there would be a difficulty, and that, if Ellington ever struck him or began a difficulty, he would kill him. Monroe talked a great deal, and witness paid but little attention to him, passing it lightly by. He showed no weapons in this conversation; can't remember any thing further; can't tell just when this conversation occurred; don't remember how long before the killing."

Cross examined:—"Don't remember how many were in the store when Monroe came in and commenced talking about the Ellingtons; Monroe said, in this conversation, he had heard they were going to tar and feather him; and he further stated that he had said what he had said that it might go to Mr. Ellington. Bledsoe said he was the last man that would take it. Monroe said the Ellingtons had made some threats against him, but witness don't remember just what they were. Monroe said he would do something, but witness don't remember what, if Ellington did so and so to him. This was sometime before the affray, but witness don't remember the precise time. It was before witness went to Springfield, which was about the first of October, but can't say how long before.'

By counsel for the prisoner:—"Didn't Monroe say, in that conversation, all he asked of them was to be let alone?"

Witness:—"I don't remember his saying so then, but he has told me that since the conversation."

J. V. Brown.—"Heard Monroe a month or so before the affray, one Sunday, talking of Mrs. Ellington. He said she was a d—d whore, a d—d thief, and a d—d liar; that Mr. Ellington and Jim were both cowards; that he intended to provoke them, and, if they resisted, shoot them down. He said if they insinuated that he lied he would shoot them down. Witness did not see any weapons. Monroe spoke of a conversation that Byrd Monroe and he had had with Mr. Ellington in reference to something which occurred at Wabash Point. Have heard Monroe make other similar threats at other times; have heard him say something about giving any one fifty dollars to get Jim Ellington in a fuss, but is not positive about it."

Cross examined by counsel for prisoner:—"Did not Monroe say he would give fifty dollars, with reference to the report that he was to be tarred and feathered?"

Witness:—"Monroe did say they were going to tar and feather him, and that he would give fifty dollars if they would undertake it. This conversation occurred a week or so before the State Fair. Monroe and wife were living together at the time of the affray, between him and Ellington."

JOHN MORTON.—"Had heard no particular threats, and knew nothing particularly about the affair."

Mr. Ficklin, for the prosecution, stated he had had no conversation with the witness, and asked him if he knew for what he was called?

The witness did not and was directed to leave the stand.

DENNIS F. HANKS.—"Lives over the drugstore; has heard Monroe many times speak of the Ellington family very improperly, but heard him make threats but once. He said he wished some of his friends would get Ellington out so that he could kill him; this was some three or four weeks before the killing; did not remember having heard him make threats at any other time. Prisoner was very much excited when he spoke of killing Ellington. Witness knew Mr. Ellington before he was married; has heard Monroe speak of Mrs. Ellington in a way a gentleman should not, but don't remember his words. He never said much about Mr. Ellington, but that he blamed Mrs. Ellington more about their difficulties."

MRS. HANKS.—"Lives over the drugstore. Has heard Monroe make threats; he was generally excited; he said, if Ellington crossed his path he would kill him; said he wished somebody would tell Ellington of this, and that if Ellington would come out he would kill him, and that he wanted to kill him. He seemed at times to be drinking and perfectly crazy."

Cross examined:—"Heard these threats a good time before the affray, some six or eight weeks; never heard any subsequent to the coming together of Monroe and wife after their separation."

J. B. Bledsoe.—"Don't remember ever to have heard Monroe threaten to kill Ellington. Have heard him say he was a s–n of a b—h, a d—d old s–n of a b—h. Witness has known him three or four years, and during that time Monroe has carried arms. Witness has seen his little white-handled pistols."

The prosecution having rested their case at this point, the first witness called for the defense was

Dumas Van Deren.—"Witness was in the street, and, hearing the report of a pistol in Byrd Monroe's store, ran in. Saw Ellington on a man who was on the floor; witness thought it was Byrd Monroe; the man was wheezing. Witness exclaimed, 'For God's sake, don't let him kill the man!' and ran up and took hold of Ellington. Mr. Ellington looked up at witness and said, 'Don't take me off; he has shot me, let me kill him!' The man under Ellington was then calling out, 'Murder! take him off!' Witness did not succeed in taking him off this time, and it was just about this time that the second pistol was fired. Witness took hold of Ellington, who then yielded to him, and witness saw that he was shot and the clothes on his breast burning. Ellington walked over to his office. The shot seemed a smothered one. It was a few seconds from the time witness first took hold of him before he finally took him off. The second pistol was fired sometime after witness got into the store. Ellington appeared very much excited, and seemed to be beating or choking Monroe."

Cross examined:—"When witness first took hold of Ellington, the latter looked up to him and said, 'Don't take me off; he has shot me, let me kill him!' Witness did not see the pistol at all. Monroe hallooed before the second pistol was fired. Don't know when Ellington's grasp was loosened; did not see Ellington have hold on Monroe's hand. Monroe was breathing as if he was dying. Did not see where Ellington had hold of Monroe, but heard Monroe make a noise as though he was strangling. There was not much done after the second pistol was fired."

Dr. Henry.—"Was sent for to see Monroe some time after the affray; was called to see his eye; it seemed to be badly gouged or scratched; it was not much swollen then, but was considerably so when I next saw him; saw some bruises on his forehead."

George Rupert.—"Don't know much about this matter; was in his grocery and some one came in and said there had been a fight in Monroe's store. Witness went over to the store. Monroe had no hat on; I saw a hat over back of the counter; George Monroe picked it up and handed it to the prisoner who put it on; the hat was eight or ten feet from the end on the west side."

Dr. Ferguson—"The first ball struck the upper part of Ellington's forehead and then ranged upward and outward, cutting the skin and passing off without inflicting serious injury. Mr. Ellington died the ninth day after he was shot from the effect of his wounds."

William Gilman.—"Saw the parties a short time before the affray sitting in the west door of the court-house, and observed nothing angry between them at that time. Supposed they had made up, and was glad to see it."

James McCrory.—"Monroe was brought into my office directly after the affray. His left eye was pretty badly gouged and he had some marks on his throat which he said smarted. Ellington was as stout as Monroe and witness both; he was a very stout man, indeed."

Mr. Cole.—"Was in the street, and, hearing a pistol fired, ran into Byrd Monroe's store; saw the parties on the floor, Ellington having Monroe under his arm. Heard somebody say, 'Part them!' but, as witness did not know how many more pistols were to be fired, he didn't go up. The second pistol was fired while Ellington held Monroe under his arm. As witness stepped in, the second pistol went off and the man under Ellington made a noise as if he were choking. Did not hear anybody say, 'Take him off!'

Never saw either of the parties before or since. Don't know whether the prisoner here is the man or not, but supposes he is."

Cross examined:—"As witness got there, the prisoner was on the floor, near the counter when the second pistol was fired. Was standing before Winchester & Smith's hardware store when the first pistol was fired."

It was here announced to the court that the evidence on that side was exhausted, and the prosecution not desiring to offer any further testimony the court adjourned until the afternoon.

The argument began on Thursday afternoon and lasted until 5 o'clock, P. M., the following Saturday.

There was no report, not so much as a synopsis of the argument of counsel made at the time, and the reader must, therefore, pardon the omission in this work.

At the conclusion of the last speech for the prosecution, the instructions were read and delivered to the jury, and they were instructed to retire and consider the case. In the mean time, the court adjourned, with directions to the jury that should they agree upon a verdict to inform him of it, through the officer in charge of them, and he would take the bench to receive it.

The jury were in their room about two hours, when the ringing of the court-house bell announced the fact that they were about to return into court. Between the time of the ringing of the bell and the delivery of the verdict, what suspense there was! To the prisoner it was more awful than a fire-bell in the night to the startled citizens; or softer and sweeter than a wedding chime, to the expectant bridegroom, as his fears or hopes alternately sunk or elated his heart.

The judge took his seat on the bench and ordered the jury to be brought into court. They came into a chamber, filled with human forms, yet as silent as a vault for the dead. His honor asked if they had agreed upon a verdict. The reply was, "We have!" and the foreman of the jury said, "We, of the jury, find the prisoner guilty as charged in the indictment!"

The court addressing each juryman in turn until the question had been proposed to all, asked, "Is that your verdict?" and each of them replied, "It is!"

The court then adjourned until Monday.

MONDAY, *January* 21, 1856, 10 *o'clock*, A. M.

The court having met pursuant to adjournment, the counsel for the prisoner made a motion for a new trial. The motion was discussed by the counsel on both sides. At the conclusion of the argument the judge remarked, that one of the instructions did not read exactly as he thought it did, and, as he, at that time, had doubts of its legality, he would take until 10 o'clock the next day, to examine the law and reflect about it ; and that if he found the instruction to be erroneous, a new trial would be freely granted.

TUESDAY, *January* 22, 10 *o'clock*, A. M.

The court met and the prisoner was placed at the bar. His honor remarked that if the counsel in the case had no other suggestion to make in reference to the motion for a new trial, he was ready now to dispose of it. Nothing being said, the court proceeded to give the result of his investigations, and concluded by remarking that, as the instruction given, was, in his opinion, legal, the motion would be overruled, and if the prisoner or his counsel had nothing to say to the contrary, he would proceed to pass the sentence of the law. Having been informed that the prisoner had nothing to say, the court proceeded in this way to pronounce

THE SENTENCE.—"It now only remains for me to pass the sentence of the law upon you. That sentence is, that you be remanded to jail to be kept in safe custody until the 15th day of next February, upon which day, between the hours of 10 A. M. and 2 P. M., you will be taken hence, by the sheriff, to some convenient spot, and there hanged by the neck until you are dead! May the Lord have mercy in your soul!"

Immediately after the sentence had been passed upon him, the prisoner was remanded to jail, and the court adjourned.

It was Monroe's intention to have delivered the following speech when he should be brought up to receive the sentence. At the earnest solicitation of his counsel, however, he omitted to pronounce it. It was afterward published, under his directions, at Paris, and circulated through the country. We give it without alteration as one of the parts of the melancholy drama, believing that the reader is entitled to a hearing of the whole case, and that it may greatly serve in the elucidation of the subject.

MONROE'S SPEECH.

SIR:—YOUR HONOR—

GENTLEMEN AND LADIES—I arise before you, for the first time in my life, to attempt to make a speech, and if I should blunder, or seem to be confused and agitated, let it be attributed to its true cause, to the natural agitation of the young and inexperienced speaker, and not to my present unfortunate position, or to fear. I do not expect or intend to make a finished speech. Such is not my province, for I am neither practiced nor experienced in the art. I simply wish to say a few words to you, as the last evidence of a dying man. I wish now to take *my* place on the stand as a *witness* in this case, and give in *my* testimony for the sake of truth and posterity when I am gone; and to enter up before this court, this people, the world and before high Heaven, my solemn protest against this awful mockery!

"On the 19th day of October last, I was arrested and cast into prison, on a charge of the murder of Nathan Ellington, my father-in-law. The excitement was great; so great, that, by the advice of my counsel, I was not present at the examination, a circumstance, which, however necessary and prudent, I shall ever regret. My counsel was forced there to *pledge himself not to change the venue!* the mob threatening that if I ever attempted it, I should be mobbed and murdered anyhow; that I should be tried here, and even if cleared, they, the mob, would hang me, whether I be innocent, or whether I be guilty! A pleasant and agreeable prospect, truly! Even thus early the counsel for the prosecution betrayed a knowledge of the weakness of their case, and that if I was ever tried out of this county I would be most surely acquitted. From the first I have been denied even the common privileges of the law. Now, it does seem to me that the law which can not protect a man, should not condemn him. Laws should be made to protect the innocent as well as to punish the guilty: and no man should be tried by a law for his life, liberty or property, unless that law can protect him while he is a prisoner. For weeks after I was committed to prison, I was threatened by a mob. The forces were to be collected even from other counties. Cut off so suddenly from the world, and shut out from the sweet sun-light of day; deprived, at once, of liberty and the presence and society of my friends; denied even the dear sweet privilege of being with my wife and child, and the natural endearments of love and the joys and delights of home and domestic peace and happiness, I grew impatient of restraint and confinement, and, contrary to the advice of my counsel, called a court that I might have either a speedy trial, or a change of venue, as might seem best; and that, if compelled to change the venue, my trial might come on at the usual time in the spring instead of having to be laid over until fall. The laws of my country gave me a right to a change of venue, or to put off my trial, as I chose, but, in this case, both have been denied me by the mob. All of this time I had no power of course to meet and mingle with the world or to hear and answer any of the charges made against me.

"The court came on. My witnesses, the most important ones, at least, were not here and could not be here in time. The excitement was still so great that I was at once advised to apply for a change of venue. This the mob again refused to allow; and my counsel, having been forced by the mob to pledge himself never to change the venue, had to go out of the case, or seem to do so, at least as far as this court and county were concerned. But my friends, who attended to matters for me, employed Thomas F. Marshall, of Kentucky, to defend me. Owing, however, to the condition of the Ohio River, he was unable to reach here. I then concluded, by Linder's advice, to put the trial off until Spring, and then change the venue if necessary. On Tuesday morning, however, I was informed, by Linder and the sheriff, that there was a band of ruffians and murderers in the town, with a drum and flying colors, determined to murder me if I attempted either to change venue or put off my trial. Again, I suffered myself to be overruled by my *friends*, and consented to a trial, rather the *outside form of one*, and the result has been as all predicted, and as all knew it would be. I was, of course, convicted and now stand before you ready to receive the sentence.

"Be it so! I can meet my fate with a smile, for my heart is at peace and my conscience is clear. I have my faults like other men. I am a child of impulse, as all who know me can testify; and, when excited, apt to speak harshly and threaten my best friend—and five minutes after ask his pardon and entrust him with the dearest secrets of my heart. But, in all of this affair, whatever errors I have committed have been caused and brought on by that love and adherence to those very feeling and principles which all good and true men hold most sacred and dear—pride of character, independence, love of courage and honor. I may have been, perchance, foolish and imprudent. I may have been too hasty and impatient in resenting a wrong and returning an insult, too open in my manner, and rash and unguarded in my speech and deportment; yet, I know that my motives have been good and my intentions pure. My conscience tells me that I am far more unfortunate than criminal, far more sinned against than sinning. I regard both Ellington and myself as rather the victims of circumstances, and the malice and machination of others, than to any faults of our own.

"The world is ever ready to pull down and trample upon the unfortunate, and there are those who now triumph over me and gloat upon my misfortunes, who are far more guilty in *His* eyes than I am. They have succeeded in bringing desolation and ruin upon happy homes and hearts, and grief and sorrow to loving hearts that never wronged them—for which they yet shall answer terribly in time or in eternity.

"There are always spirits in any community so low and groveling in their natures, that they can not rise above the base feelings of malice and envy, and who can not bear to see another prosper, particularly if he is so unfortunate asto be poor, and too proud and independent to stoop to fawn upon and flatter them—without seeking, by every means in their power, however low and base, to abuse and injure them, stooping even to the foulest slander and lies of the darkest hue to every thing mean and servile to accomplish their object, which, when accomplished, does them no good, except to gratify their depraved minds, passions and appetites.

"There is always a feverish desire in the public, particularly among the lower and baser classes, to see a fellow being suffer, and to convict him, *right* or *wrong*, when once in the strong clutches of the law—a kind of fiendish pleasure and excitement in seeing a neighbor fall degraded. It is a spirit worthy the scorn and contempt of all honest men. 'T is the same fell spirit that prompted the Jews to cry out against our Saviour, "Crucify him! Crucify him!" Let a man be but once unfortunate, and the world is ever ready to pull him down, to sink him lower and lower, and to *stamp* and trample upon him while he is weak and helpless. Who does not know and has not seen, even in the canine species, that when once poor *Tray* is down he is set upon and torn to pieces by the whole pack of hounds? Alas! for me, like poor Tray, I have sometimes been caught in bad company.

"Such has been the evident determination in my case from the first. I blame not the judge; for, though the old and valued friend of the deceased, he has conducted this trial with a fairness and moderation for which I thank him—from my inmost heart I thank him. I blame not the counsel of the opposite side; two of them, at least, have shown great delicacy and forbearance. My counsel has done all that could be done—all that man could do, and more perchance, than any other man could have done. But all, of course, was in vain. An angel from heaven—a messenger from God—could not have changed the decision in this case. What counsel—what law—what court could conquer or govern a *mob*? What jury could dare bring in a verdict of acquittal under such *instructions*, and in the face of such a mass of frowning brows and scowling countenances, ferociously demanding blood to have their blood-thirsty appetites appeased? Indeed, I suppose it was a fortunate thing for me and for the honor and the memory of the county forever that I was not acquitted by that jury, for I would have been *instantly murdered* by a band of ruffians and murderers—God knows who or wherefrom—who were there (so 't is said by the officers themselves) in the court-room, ready and prepared with a rope to murder me if not convicted of a capital offense. My God! can Coles county be sunk so low, so lost to all morality, decency and honor? Whence comes this hord of lawless scoundrels? Are they of this county? Are there any respectable men and citizens even of *his* friends and relatives, among them? I hope not. The common murderer who goes out at midnight and raises his *single* arm against his sleeping foe, and plunges the assassin dagger into the heart of his unconscious victim, is a brave and honorable man—a Christian—when compared to him who leagues with a mob, composed perhaps of hundreds, to murder a single, unarmed, weak and helpless prisoner, already in the merciless hand of the law! Of all crimes, of all murders this is the most foul and horrible—the most hellish and cowardly!

"I feel indebted to, and indeed thank *all* of the counsel for the prosecution, for their moderation and fairness, except, be it *forever* remembered, except the Honorable Orlando Obediah Bustamente De La Ficklin, Esq., who seems to have been specially hired and paid to lie and slander, rail and abuse in this case. In truth, he seems fully competent to the task! His conscience must indeed be seared, and his heart hardened, for he seemed utterly regardless of all human sympathy and feelings—of all truth and honor! Truly, as he remarked, there was but '*one heart*' in all that family that ever received and welcomed me. True it is too, *that* heart has never failed me! never faltered or fallen from me! '*Tis mine yet! all mine!* notwithstanding he so pathetically alluded to the 'beautiful, worthy and accomplished young lady who had so unfortunately married the prisoner!' Beautiful she is, and worthy, far more worthy than beautiful! Worthy! aye far worthier than such a soul as his could ever honor or appreciate! Go to *her* to-day, and ask her whom she censures in all this sad affair, whom *she* thinks the guilty parties? Go, ask her if she ever blamed me even for an instant or ever had cause to regret our union? and if she does not answer in my favor, freely and fully, and say that the love and trust that is burning in her heart for me this day, even as I stand here convicted of the murder of her father, is glowing with a far higher, purer and holier, more lasting, deep, fond, confiding and tender, deathless and undying love, than it was upon our bridal morn—*then, I am a murderer!*

"Go, ye who seek for vengeance, to those who have done this deed! Ye who are crying 'blood for blood!' and demanding a victim, go, if ye would find and punish the guilty parties, go seek them elsewhere. *His blood is not upon my hand!* Oh! if ye really wish to know who are the *true criminals*, who are his true murderers, then go, in God's name, I'd bid you go, seek them nearer home; you will find them *there!* Ay! as my counsel said, 'there is an under current and a mystery in all this affair, which the world may never know—but had *her* evidence been admitted here all would have been as open and as bright as day. But God forbid that I, even in self-defense, should drag out the secret of this family difficulty. Some day all may and all will be known; and long after I am gone, when the green grass shall wave above my lowly tomb, when the trees shall have budded and blossomed and the leaves withered and fallen again and again, and when, one by one, all those present shall have passed away, after long years, 't will be said, 'Dolph Monroe fell unjustly!' that 'he *was foully and cruelly murdered* and by those who were the guilty parties, by those who have caused and brought on this whole affair—and by those who have hunted him down and sworn his life away.'

"But a tone, a word, a memory of my fate shall hang forever upon the viewless air, with a curse, a bitter curse, and haunt them throughout all time and eternity; wring their false hearts, shake their craven souls, weigh down their guilty consciences with remorse and regret, and drag them down to hell forever.

"On the 12th day of December, 1853, I was married to Nannie Ellington, with whom I lived most happily, and with whom I could live most happily forever, for she is truly amiable, good and pure —worthy of all man's best affection, all love and praise. But, alas! difficulties soon arose, dark and fierce, between her relatives and mine; and finally between her and mine, and her relatives and myself. "What they were, I will not now state or drag to light. Suffice it to say that between her and myself all was peace, harmony, confidence and love;—and, right here, I will state a fact which may take some by surprise and seem strange, yet it is no less true than strange; notwithstanding it was sworn to here in court in evidence and the world regarded it so, *there never was a separation between me and my wife.* She was at her father's house just a week, but 't was a pre-arranged affair between us, known and understood between ourselves. I only mention this, however, as an evidence of the fallacy and frailty of human knowledge and testimony—for it matters not either way.

"Numerous threats have been sworn to here, some true and some false—all false, in the words and spirit with which remembered and delivered. I never made any threats against Ellington except on the condition of being attacked by him and in self-defense; and as warnings in answer to threats of *their's*. I often said I did not blame Ellington so much as I did others, and *always* said, I only asked to be let alone; and in threatening, I usually used the word 'them,' instead of 'him,' as all know.

"On the night of the 18th of October last, James Ellington and Byrd Monroe had a quarrel about some accounts, during which the young man, I suppose, got into a tight place, and, coward-like, shuffled the affair off upon his father's shoulders—but for which base and dastardly act his father would have been upon the earth to-day. My name too was called upon that night by the young man during the quarrel, and I was sent for and hunted up, but took no part in the difficulty. The next morning, the 19th of October, and the one upon which the fatal tragedy occurred, I was in the drugstore and was giving an account of the manner in which Byrd Monroe had talked to James Ellington, mimicing Byrd Monroe's voice and gestures, when he told Jim that he 'could find twenty or fifty men who could swear that he could not tell the truth;' and I remarked that *they* were going to get together that morning and I supposed that they would settle the matter when Jimmie would be in a tight place again, for I did not believe his father had stated what he said he did. Mr. Ellington's name was mentioned but the one time and then in that way. Here, Mr. Wilkinson, who seems to have got his evidence from some book, and memorized it for the occasion and repeated it by rote with a gladiatorial air and swagger, was, to say the least of it, *grossly* mistaken. Indeed, his whole testimony was a tissue of *mistakes*, from which the prosecution wove a web of very plausible but flimsy circumstances against me. Whether he has done this thing for the 'thirty pieces,' or from hate, malice or envy, or, merely from a blood-thirsty appetite, I can not say. According to his own evidence, however, he went there, not to prevent a difficulty but to see one, and to eat up George Monroe alive; and yet, this man, this California gambler and faro-dealer; this butcher, who by his own account has murdered a dozen men while there for merely disputing his word and asserting their rights when he was swindling them at the faro-table; this professed gambler who lives by enticing unwary young men to the card-table to swindle them out of their money—this man, this perjurer, who has sworn my life away, has been styled by the prosecution, '*a respectable young man!*'

"But enough of him! God and his conscience for it! From the drugstore, I started to go to dinner, as we ate very early at my boarding-house; and Mr. Moore not being at home, I was hastening to see that Mrs. Moore had sufficient wood cut, as I had sent a boy to cut some. I will here state that I had a horse and buggy in readiness to go with my wife to Cunningham's that evening, and would have gone in the morning but for the absence of Mr. Moore, my wife not feeling inclined to leave Mrs. Moore alone. When I started to dinner, as was my usual custom, I took a straight and direct line from the drugstore to the house, not following the side walks. I did not see Mr. Ellington until within a few feet of him, and then I perceived he was very angry. God knows what his son Jim had gone home that night and told him; none may ever know until the secrets of all hearts are known, but this much I do know, that he had told him something of his affair of the night before with Byrd Monroe—in which all said he was wrong, but of that I know nothing—which made him very angry with both Byrd Monroe and myself; and when I met him he had been once to Byrd Monroe's to see him, and was on his way there again. Seeing him, and feeling certain from his manner that Jim had told him of the affair, I laughingly remarked to him:

"I suppose Jim told you of his *muss* last night. They sent for me and hunted me up, but I did not see that I had any thing to do with it—I only laughed at them.

"He raised his cane and said:—'Yes, you have something to do with it, you puppy! Byrd Monroe has been lying some time and you have denied things you said to him.'

"I stepped back several steps, and told him not to strike me with his cane, that Byrd Monroe would not say so. He replied that he would. I again asserted that he would not. He then asked me to go with him to the store. I hesitated, and he again

said, 'Come on! 'come along!' Thus urged the second time, I went. Byrd Monroe was not there. I remarked to Ellington that I did not see why he should blame me for every lie that he heard, that if, as he said, Byrd and John Monroe lied, it was no business of mine—but he and they for it; that I knew nothing about this scrape, cared nothing about it, nor did I want to know any thing about it, and I did not see why in the h—ll I was dragged into it. He then said, 'I have no doubt but that you have told forty lies about it.' I commenced to make a kind reply, but passion got the better of my tongue and reason, and I said, 'Oh! well, now, if I have told forty lies, you have told sixty.' At this time he was standing with his back to the east counter, leaning with his elbow on the show-case, with his cane in his hand grasped about the middle. I was standing by the west counter, which is not so long by six or eight feet and below the pile of goods on the end, at least ten or twelve feet from him. Upon my reply, he said, 'Ha! you trifling puppy, you talk to me in that way!' Throwing up *both* arms, he ran at me; I stepped back several steps as he came; catching me with his right hand by the collar, and by the throat with his left, his cane striking me upon the left hand, as I threw it up to ward off his attack, skinning it considerably and striking me smartly upon the forehead. He then choked me back upon the counter when I fired the first shot at him, or rather toward where I supposed he was, for I was choked so far back with my head over the counter that I could not see him at the time. Mr. Wilkinson states that he saw my pistol in my right hand partly drawn. Again 'the honorable and respectable young man' was mistaken. My hand did not touch it, nor was it drawn till I was upon the counter. He then threw me upon the floor, with my face downward, springing upon me, choking and gouging me rapidly. I could then have drawn my second pistol and shot him again, but a thought of my wife and child flashed over me, and I called out several times for help, when I heard Eastin say in answer to my call, 'Stamp him to death! stamp him to death! d—n him!' I did not know until afterward, that any one was offering to take him off at all. In a second after, I called again twice, for help, when I heard Ellington say to some one, 'No! no! don't touch me! let me kill him!' I was then choked almost to death; my eyes were nearly gouged out, and with this threat ringing in my ears, in despair, with a desperate effort, I arose to my knee and fired the second and last shot, when we were *instantly separated.*

"The second pistol was never drawn until the instant 't was fired. And, here, again, Mr. Wilkinson was mistaken. Ellington never had hold either of my hands or wrists, but on the contrary, I held his hands from my eyes and throat, while I called upon the crowd 'to take him off,' and God knows had that assistance been given when called for, or had not Ellington said he would *kill* me, that second shot would never have been fired. I could have shot him before, but I did not wish to do so. Even then the thought of my wife and child prevented me, and I wished the difficulty to end without any more harm being done. But, alas! fate willed it otherwise, and he is gone and I am here! Why, I would ask of those who best may answer; why, why was Ellington's last dying statement not brought forward here? I asked it; my friends asked it; my counsel asked it; why was it not here? *The counsel for the prosecution refused to permit it.* Let the fact speak for itself! It is awfully significant.

"From the first of this affair, I have been hunted down with blood-hound ferocity, by false witnesses, envy, malice and hate. May God forgive all those who have sought my fall as freely as I do! Rather, far rather, aye ten thousand times rather had I stand here to-day, *their victim*, than to live on, even for ages, with the awful weight of agony, regret and remorse which time must and will surely bring home to their hearts and consciences.

"But a few more words and I have done. Soon this heart shall cease to beat and the tones of this voice be hushed, and the places which have known me 'know me no more forever!' My place by the side of my friends, of my mother and sister, my wife and child, shall be left vacant, never more to be filled again on earth. Be it so! This solemn farce is over, this awful mockery is ended, and I fall a victim to popular fury and mobocracy! The victim stands before you ready to receive his sentence; prepared for the sacrifice—*I am ready!* Cut off in the morning of life, so early, so unfortunately, so unjustly, with all so fair and bright before me, with the future opening up so many sweet views and visions of joy and happiness, peace, prosperity, fame and honor—a happy husband and a father—I fall without a murmur! The lamb is dumb before the altar. I ask not your sympathy; I need it not. 'T is the sympathy of the tiger for his prey, of the wolf for the lamb which he devours—and 't is literally the sympathy of the mob for their victim.

"Oh! if there is any consolation in death after a calm heart, clear conscience, faith and hope, 't is the thought of leaving this foul nest of liars and slanderers! 'T is hard, it is true, to die so young, so loving and beloved! 'T is true, I had rather live, for there are those whom 't is worse, far worse, and more bitter than death itself to leave; and *I am no stoic!* Though calm, my heart is sad, aye very sad; sad for him who has gone before; sad for my friends, and sad for my own sad fate and early doom, so undeserved; and sad—oh! how sad!—for an old and infirm mother, who leans upon me for support; and sadder, far sadder still, for my poor, broken-hearted, unhappy widowed wife and helpless orphan child—for her, my wife, with all her fond affections crushed and bright hopes blasted—for her! in her sad and unfortunate position—and how sad and unfortunate her position *is* the world may never know; for, in the midst of her kindred, she is in the midst of her foes! For her, in her desolation and woe, my heart bleeds, my spirit shrinks, and my head is bowed in grief to the dust.

"But though my heart is sad, I stand here before you to-day with no pale face of fear, no shrinking form of terror. This frail body you may hew from the earth and trample upon my dust when I am gone; but my heart you can not change—my soul you can not reach; my spirit you can not conquer! Far better, and higher, and holier men than I have fallen, and fallen far more ignominiously and unjustly. *Our* Saviour died upon the cross, and kings and princes have perished on the scaffold. I fall, but I will fall proudly! Strong in the conciousness of my own innocence, knowing the purity of my own motives and intentions, I go with a calm heart and a firm and even soul to meet my God!

"Across the dark waters of that mysterious stream which flows between time and eternity, I will 'paddle my own lone canoe,' to the unseen shores of that Great Beyond—that dread unknown, that awful world of the solemn hereafter, fully satisfied and believing that *his shade*, who has gone before, freed from the frailties of *human nature* and the vail which darkens *mortal* eyes, will there read my heart aright and be among the first to meet and extend to me the hand of welcome in the spiritland!

"You have rendered your verdict which posterity and heaven shall sit upon and *reverse*. But from an earthly court and an earthly tribunal, I appeal to that court and that tribunal before which we all must one day appear; and I summon you now to meet me there, and answer each and all of you for this foul deed of murder and wrong! Before Him who sees the sparrow fall, who numbers our hairs upon our heads; before the Great Searcher of human hearts and souls, we'll meet again! To that tribunal I now appeal—to that tribunal, I am now going. That court must soon pass upon my heart and deeds. But there, with God for my judge, Christ for my advocate. and angels for my jurors, I have nought to fear!"

Amazement must take possession of the mind of every reader, when one by one the circumstances of this extraordinary affair are developed. From the very beginning there seems to have been a determination on the part of those who in the end participated in the horrid tragedy about to be described, that neither the acquittal of a jury nor the executive clemency should save the prisoner from the bloody doom to which they intend to consign him. He was not allowed to be present at the court of inquiry by which he was formally committed to jail to await his trial. When restive at the confinement to which he was subject, and asserting that no jury could convict him of a capital offense, he asked a court to be called that he might have a fair and impartial hearing, it was announced to him in the most unmistakable manner that the mob had determined that he should not have a change of venue and that he should not be acquitted; that if he succeeded in procuring either he should be instantaneously murdered. When the court met it was filled with an excited and infuriated populace. Ropes, more than one, had been prepared with which to hang him, provided his application for a change of venue should prove successful.

Overawed by the display and threats of this determination, what could he, single and a prisoner, do against the crowd that stood around him? He was compelled to submit and to suffer himself to go through with the form of a trial which he new must result in his conviction, rather than on the spot to be hanged by the mob. We have seen how this trial began, proceeded, and how it has now concluded in a sentence of death against him. Few situations are entirely without hope. There opened up to him but two prospects of escape from his unhappy situation. These were, on the one hand, that the supreme court of the State might reverse the sentence for irregularity in the proceedings and order a new trial of his case; or, if that should fail, that the Governor of the State, upon a proper representation of the facts, could scarcely refuse to pardon him, or, at least, delay the execution of the sentence affording him thereby an opportunity more effectually to make some shift to relieve himself entirely.

The first hope soon failed him, for on an application to the supreme court to reverse the sentence of the inferior one by which he had been tried, it was refused.

The last hope was now in an application to the Governor. It was made by the two persons who of all the inhabitants of earth were fittest to present it—the prisoner's mother and his wife. The one, upon whose bosom he had slept in his innocent childhood; and the other, who had folded him to her heart in the first warm gush of womanhood, with the fond devotion of a young and loving wife. The one pleaded for the son whom she had hoped would be her staff in her declining years—for whom she had offered a thousand petitions, and whom, in the midst of his darkness, she loved more fondly than ever; and the other interceded for the father of her child and the husband of her woman's heart. Unmindful of the fact that all her kindred were arrayed against her, and that he for whose pardon she implored had been convicted of the murder of her own father, she left nothing undone in behalf of her husband and applied herself to his cause with unswerving devotion. The darkest picture has some ray of light, and often, in the darkest night, some bright star appears to tinge with silver the edges of the cloud through which it breaks. How beautiful! how worthy of all admiration appears the devotion of this young and devoted woman! Her love for her husband burns as brightly as burns the lamp, which in some countries is lighted by love and watched by memory above the tombs of departed friends!

A respite was granted by the Governor who extended the time of the execution from the 15th of February until the 15th of May.

No sooner had intelligence of this action on the part of the Governor reached Charleston, than the community was thrown into the wildest excitement. Threats were loud and furious. To an observing man it was very apparent that the clemency of the highest officer of the State found no response in the hearts of the excited populace, and that the days of the prisoner were not only numbered but that the number was fewer than those allowed by the respite.

The end of this fearful affair was discribed, by the messenger who was dispatched to Charleston with the respite, in a letter to the Missouri Republican. Coming as it does from an individual wholly impartial, it is supposed to be entirely worthy of credit and is given in the writer's own language. The time referred to in the first line being the 14th of February, 1856.

"About six o'clock crowds began coming in; about four hundred came in on the evening train, and about one thousand persons in all were present. It was rumored that the prisoner would be taken out that night and hung, but such was not the case.

"At an early hour next morning, Friday the 15th, the day upon which Monroe was sentenced to be hung, crowds of people were seen coming into Charleston in wagons, sleds, and by every means of conveyance. In these crowds were women and children, who were coming 'to see the fun,' as they said.

"At about 11 o'clock, it was estimated that four or five thousand persons were present and assembled in and around the square. At about 10 o'clock, I saw the crowd moving toward the court-house, in the center of the square, where I learned that speeches were to be made, and being desirous of hearing what was said, I passed up and stood close to the stand to be occupied by the speaker.

"A man named Cunningham, who it is understood is the ringleader of the mob, and who could control it as he desired, first mounted the stand and spoke as follows:

" 'Fellow-citizens:—I appear here as a friend of Ellington, and to inform you that a respite has been granted by the Governor, postponing the execution till the 15th of May. I have always had respect for the law. I have consulted with some of old Nathan's friends, and many of the citizens of Cole, *upon the subject of obeying the respite*, and have come to the conclusion, upon reflection, *to postpone the execution*, until the time fixed upon by his Excellency, upon the condition that the sheriff, who now stands upon my left, will chain the prisoner down, and pledge himself to be responsible for his safe keeping until the day fixed on by the Governor for his execution, and that *he shall be executed on that day*, notwithstanding his Excellency the Governor. (Loud and long cheering.) I want the Governor to understand that we, the people of Coles county, are competent to attend to our own affairs, without his interference, and that we are determined he shall not do as he previously did in a case above here. (Enthusiastic cheering.) I now move that we prepare resolutions and get up a petition, the first giving our consent to the time fixed upon by the Governor for his execution, and the second for the purpose of contradicting the many misrepresentations and falsehoods which have been sent to the Governor, upon which said misrepresentations and falsehoods he granted the respite—and to request him to SHORTEN the time for hanging.

" 'Gentlemen, these are my views, and what I am willing to submit to notwithstanding my intimate connection with the deceased, upon the ground that the sheriff will pledge himself as a man, and as sheriff of Coles county, to iron the prisoner, and that *he shall be executed on that day*. (The sheriff, standing near him, responded that he would.)

" 'Gentlemen, in saying what I have, I speak the sentiments of some of old Nathan's friends with whom I have conversed to-day, *but only a part of them*.'

" After the speech of Cunningham, a man named McNary was called upon who said, speaking of the prisoner, 'Take him out, G—d d–n him; take him out and hang him!'

After the speeches of the above named men and others, the court-house bell commenced ringing, which seemed to be a signal for an attack on the jail. The mob, inflamed and excited by the speeches they had heard, rushed *en masse* to the jail-yard, where, yelling like demons let loose from the infernal region, they began to make an attack on the north side of the jail. Some ten or fifteen minutes after they had commenced the attack, the sheriff made his appearance and addressed the mob for about two minutes, commanding them to desist, but made no appeal to the spectators to assist him in enforcing the law. The sheriff then disappeared, and made no further effort either to resist the mob or to protect the prisoner.

"The mob were about two hours in making a breach in the wall of the jail. I think not more than ten or twelve men did the actual work, but they were encouraged by a large portion of the crowd, who used every means to keep up the excitement. During all this time were heard the sounds of fife and drum amid the demoniac yells of the multitude.

"Several men who were placed in jail as a guard stood in the open windows with guns in hand, and called upon the crowd to assist in the work and to take the prisoner out and hang him. Some of these men were placed there by the sheriff. The others were placed there by other parties for the purpose of watching the movements of the prisoner and preventing any escape. One man displayed out of the window a portrait of Monroe's wife—the daughter of Ellington—and called upon the crowd in a vehement manner to behold the daughter of the father the prisoner had murdered. It is proper here to state that Monroe's wife has always sustained him in this dreadful affair.

"At times during the attack upon the jail, the excitement of the mob would die away, and I have no doubt that had the sheriff, or any other prominent citizen, made the effort, he might have succeeded in quelling the excitement and restoring order.

"I wish here to give the names of a few of those most prominent in doing the work. Wm. Hart, grocery keeper, of Charleston, principal actor in breaking the jail. This man worked at times with an ax, sledge-hammer, crowbar, etc., and when he would be exhausted he would call upon the crowd to come up and assist him in taking vengeance. Solomon Corsel, said to be a resident of Clark county, and Thomas and John Epperson were said also to be the names of some of the workers. The name of the man who displayed the portrait is Dennis Bell. The names of many others of the active participants it is said are known.

"When the breach was made large enough, the prisoner was dragged through, badly bruised and insensible amid the deafening shouts of the mob, who immediately moved with him toward the square, the fife and the drum in the mean time sounding. The crowd pressed around and it would have been impossible to know the position of the prisoner, had it not been designated by one who carried a long staff.

"The mob then proceeded to the public square, with the intention of there hanging the prisoner, and thus completing the hellish transaction; but about this time I noticed a prominent citizen edge his way through the crowd with the intention, as I supposed, of addressing the mob, but in this I was disappointed. However the mass commenced moving toward the square, and the cry immediately arose, 'To the woods! to the woods!'

"Immediately the mass moved with the prisoner to the woods. After proceeding about half a mile southwest of the square another halt was made, and those most active pressed the crowd back and succeeded in making a ring in which some six or seven held the prisoner. In the middle of the ring was a tree against which a ladder was placed, on which a man ascended with an ax, with which he trimmed off the smaller branches. The rope was now made fast to the tree, and all things appeared ready for the blackest outrage which has at any time been perpetrated by any people, much less those who have claims to civilization.

"During all the time the prisoner appeared insensible of what was going on, being unable to sustain himself alone. He appeared like a man who had taken poisonous drugs which had taken effect upon him. He did not seem to heed the crowd, but would occasionally laugh in a wild and insane manner.

"All being now prepared for the execution of their purpose, the mob seem for the first time to reflect upon what they were about to do. All was silent, yet no one dared to assert the right of the prisoner and the supremacy of the law: could such an one have been found the dreadful end might have been avoided.

"Again the cry was raised, 'Take him back to jail!' 'Will you hang a dead man?' but some demon's voice was heard saying,

'You G—d d–n cowards! are you afraid to hang him after bringing him here?' The prisoner was now placed in a wagon under the rope, and again the mob hesitated. It seemed that no one could be found blood-thirsty enough to adjust the rope to his neck. Finally, a tool in the hands of others by the name of Thomas Fleming placed the rope around the prisoner's neck while others held him up. The wagon was pulled away and the awful deed accomplished, the victim as he hung not making the least struggle.

"Sickened and disgusted with the scene, I retired, and by the next train left the town. I heard, on my return from Terre Haute, that the body was taken down by the mob who had not yet satiated their brutal vengeance and carried in a wagon twice round the public square of the town as in triumph of their disgraceful deed. Upon the appeal of the sister of Monroe his body was surrendered to his friends for burial.

"Thus ended one of the most hellish outrages that ever disgraced Illinois. May its history never be marked by another.

"In addition to the above, we will add, that it can be proved by two or more respectable citizens of Edgar county, as we are informed, that previous to the trial of Monroe a man stated that he wanted to get upon the jury for the purpose of hanging the scoundrel (meaning Monroe); and it can also be proven that the same man was on the jury! It can also be proven that two, or one, in particular, of the witnesses for the prosecution are men of doubtful character, being professional blacklegs.

"It is not our present purpose to inquire whether Monroe had the full benefit of the law—whether he had a fair trial—but it is our purpose to inquire where were the men—the *prominent* and influential men of Coles county, that they should let such a damnable outrage blacken not only the town of Charleston, not only Coles county, but cast a stain upon our whole State?

"Where was the sheriff of Coles county, that he should not do his duty and uphold the sanctity of the law! that he should let a mob murder a man in the broad light of day in this free and common country, without making scarcely the slightest resistance, without calling upon the law-abiding people to assist him, when his call would have been responded to by numbers?

"We confess that in all the annals of barbarity and crime we have never known of, never read of such inhuman brutality as has recently been perpetrated in the hitherto fair county of Coles."

No comment upon this unvarnished narrative is necessary. The wild excitement of the mob added to and supported by the sound of martial music; the inflammatory speeches of the mob orators, who, while pretending to allay, really sought to increase the madness and ferocity of the crowd; the display of Mrs. Monroe's portrait from the prison window; the wild hurrah with which the brutal industry of the assailants of the jail was kept alive and with which their successful attempt was hailed; the timidity, to say the least of it, of the sheriff; the shrinking even of that crowd of blood-thirsty men at the thought of the murder they were about to commit; their wavering and hesitation; the prisoner's helplessness; his frantic appearance, and loud insane laugh;—the final and fearful exclamation of that human fiend who called for his execution; the murdered man exhausted, fainting, and senseless before the knot was tied, and then dying without a struggle; and then the horrible and savage delight with which his lacerated body was dragged about the public square—what need is there to dwell upon such sights as these? Already is the mind of the reader amazed that such a thing could be perpetrated in the midst of civilized life, in this age of the world, and at the recital his heart has sickened and his blood run fiercely through its channels.

He is now beyond the reach of human power. His soul has returned to Him who gave it with its sins, we hope, in a great measure expiated by the cruel ordeal by which it was released. As in life he had retained through all variations of his checkered fortunes the love of his wife and mother and of his sister and her husband, so they were not unmindful of him in his death. With broken hearts they took charge of his remains after the mob had expended its fury upon them and bore them back to Kentucky. There, amid the places which were so dear to him in youth, his ashes await the general resurrection. Near the shores of the beautiful stream which ever murmured in his ear when far away from it, in a resting-place decorated in accordance with his own request, he sleeps the sleep that knows no waking!

MY PRESENT POSITION AND ITS CAUSES.

On the 12th of December, 1853, I was married to Miss Nannie Ellington, much against the will of her mother, who was so bitterly opposed to our union that she threatened to turn her daughter out of doors, if I ever came there to see her; so, of course, I never visited the house. Her only cause of opposition and hatred of me was her inveterate dislike of all the Monroe family, and no fault of mine; and, strange as it may appear, I did not even know her, and never saw her in my life, until I was introduced to her by Nannie, to ask her consent to our marriage; which she ungraciously gave, for she could not help herself. Nannie was determined, and her father willing, but *she* never forgave me, and seemed determined, from the first, to produce a separation between my wife and myself, for which end she labored unceasingly—abusing me continually, and begging Nannie to leave me, which, though she failed to effect it, has at length ended in the present unfortunate affair. May God forgive her!

Ellington himself was a good man, and meant to do right; and, but for her baneful influence, was my friend, and would have treated me well; but, misled by her and others, he became prejudiced against me—abused me and my mother very often in disgusting terms, until, finally, on the 19th day of October last (1855), he gave me the lie, and struck me; choking me back upon the counter; when I fired upon him—striking him upon the top of the head, but wounding him very slightly. He then threw me upon the floor upon my face, all the while beating, gouging, and choking me. He was a very large and stout man, able to handle three or four men of my physical strength. I called upon the crowd, several times, "to take him off," which they did not do, and which he refused to let them do. I *then*, as my last resource, to save my eyes, and to prevent being choked to death, shot him again, which resulted in his death on October 27th, eight days afterward. Had not John Eastin called out to Ellington to "stamp him to death, d–n him," after I had told the crowd to take him off, and had not Ellington refused to be taken off, I should not have shot the second time. I was arrested, and confined here in prison. My wife was then forced to go to Ellington's for a home, as I could no longer protect her, and she is now there, almost as unhappily situated as myself, for she is abused and mistreated by her mother and her family, and not allowed to have any correspondence with me, on pain of being turned out of doors; and, by her father's will, she is not an heir, unless she consents never to see me again, and gets a divorce from me. Her only resource is to accept a home there on *any* terms, as I am no longer able to provide her one or protect her; but she defies them to force her to speak ill of me, to desert me, or suffer them to speak of a divorce. My God! I feel her sorrows more than I do my own! May good angels protect, and God forever bless thee, my noble, noble, wife!

COPY OF A LETTER

WRITTEN BY MONROE TO HIS WIFE, DATED NOVEMBER 12, 1855.

Nannie:—Dear Nannie, my sweet, my noble wife, what misfortunes have come upon us; what a cruel fate is ours, rudely torn asunder in the midst of joy and happiness, peace and love. (Alas! we loved *too* well for this world—*too* well to last!) Oh, why should this sorrow have come upon us, at such a time, too, when we were and could have been so happy together; when you had just proved your love to be as deep and devoted as my own; when you had just proved your love and truth by clinging to me, even when discarded and disowned by your relations for so doing. I never knew how happy I was until then, Nannie, for I never knew before how much you loved me. I never knew how inexpressibly dear you were to me, until I thought I had lost you; nor can you ever know, until you know it in a better world than this, how well I have loved you, how well I love you now. You are all the world to me; without you and my child, without you and your love, I do not wish to live. Oh! Nannie, when I have seemed cold and harsh to you, it was only because I thought you ought to have had more confidence in me, and loved me better than all the rest of the world. If you had resented it when your friends insulted and abused me, I never would have doubted you, but loved you all the better for it. It wounded me to think you would allow them to persuade you to leave me. It wounded me to the soul, and steeled my heart to hide all its love and tenderness for you, though my *proud* heart was breaking then to own all my love, and to know that you loved me as well. Oh! Nannie, had your relatives ever treated me kindly, even as a friend; if I had been welcome even in their house; if they had shown but common politeness toward me, I could have loved them for *your* sake, and all would have been well *now*; but, alas!—why I know not—they hated me from the first. You can bear me witness, Nannie, that I never mistreated any of them, or gave them cause to abuse me. Oh! if your father and mother had come to me with kindness, I would have done any thing on earth to please them, granted any thing they asked, and done as they wished, to serve or please them. If they had not said so much about their wealth, Nannie, and my *crime* of being *poor*, but proud and independent; if they had done their duty to you as their daughter, and treated me well, at least, for your sake; then there would not have been any trouble, your father would now be alive, and we living happily together. Do not think I will justify *my* relations, Nannie, for they, too, have been to blame; we have *all*, no doubt, been more or less to blame. I have been too proud and unbending, but you can not blame me, Nannie, for refusing to let them give me any thing, after all they said about me; not only charging me with having *married you for their money*, but, also, with being a spendthrift and a drunkard; and after thier begging you to leave me, oh! why should they thus have sought, not only to make my home unhappy, but, you, too, miserable? Was this the province, the love and duty of parents? I know you do not and can not blame me, and if I had acted otherwise you could not have respected me; neither do I blame your father as much as I do others. I never thought he meant to do wrong—but, alas! your mother and the town tattlers completely poisoned his mind against me, and when you hear *all*, you will not blame *me*, Nannie, for his death. As God is my Judge, *I* did not bring on this sorrow. I wished to avoid it, but

could not. I was *forced* into it, and acted only in self-defense to the last. I am unfortunate, but not criminal; unhappy, but guilty of no crime but that the laws of God and man allow. No human being can regret the sad termination of this affair more than I do. It has surely brought more misery upon *me* and *mine* than any one else. It has torn me from my wife and child whom I loved better than life itself, and cast me into prison, where I may have to stay until spring, if I do not die before of cold and exposure. Oh! Nannie, you can not imagine what a lamp it is, lighting up the gloomy darkness of this dungeon, the thought that, though unfortunate and suffering here, you are—you will be true to me still! Now is the time, Nannie, in adversity, and trial, and trouble, for a *wife* to prove her love and devotion, and nobly, my sweet wife, have you stood the test! May you be happy, Nannie; may you find others to love you half as well as I have done, and ever shall. I want to see you and my child again. Surely your mother can not prevent your coming to see me. Come, and let me know what you intend to do, and what you wish. May God forever bless you and my child. I will try and bear this sorrow for your sakes. Farewell, until I see you again. May all good angels comfort you.

Your unfortunate, but devoted husband,

A. F. MONROE.

MY DESTINY.

"L'HOMME PROPOSE, ET DIEU DISPOSE."

Napoleon and Byron, two of the most gifted but unfortunate men on earth, both believed in destiny, and both met a sad, strange fate. Napoleon was the "child of destiny," and Byron the "sensitive plant" of misfortune. I do not quote their examples and sorrows to compare them with my own, but merely as a proof that *all*, both great and small, high and low, rich and poor, master and slave, king and subject, priest and laity, must submit, alike to *fate*, whose stern and irrevocable decrees, whether for good or evil, surround, embrace, and encircle *all*, governing and controlling our lives and actions, from the cradle to the grave.

My own life has been a curious, "a shifting scene," composed of good and evil, smiles and tears; always succeeding, and always failing, too. My life has been of extremes. My hopes and fears, thoughts and feelings, loves and hates, have always been in extreme. My whole life, my fate is but an extreme one way or other. I think, feel, act, and suffer in the extreme. Why this is I know not, I only know the fact, but can not change my nature. My good and ill luck in life, my fortunes and misfortunes, have been a succession of extremes; first extremely happy, and then extremely miserable: one hour success, and hope and joy; the next, doubt, despair and ruin. Now all this, from every thing I can see, I take to be FATE. My whole life has been what seems an accident—a succession of circumstances and accidents, call them what you will, have made me what I am, deciding all I have been, and may be hereafter, for "the end is not yet," and my fate is not quite, though so nearly fulfilled.

SOLITUDE AND REFLECTIONS.

Alone, here, shut up from the world, buried as it were in this living tomb, in silence and solitude, I have at length found time to look into my own heart and to *know myself*. Alas! in this secret examination of my own soul, I find much to deplore, much to regret. Though deeply and bitterly wronged by my savage mother-in-law, Ellington himself and family, I have not been altogether blameless, myself. Ellington, I always thought and still think, was a good and true man, and would but for his wife, have done his duty to his daughter and to me. I think and believe he meant to do right, but was led to wrong his better nature by his wife and others. As to his wife, who has been the sole originator and cause of all this trouble and affliction, I have but little to say, for words are vain and inadequate to express the foul deformity of a being so lost to humanity and heaven—a blot upon her sex, and stain to the human race. Unnatural woman and unnatural mother, God and her own conscience will haunt her, wring her wretched heart, and sink her soul to perdition with speedy, sure and dreadful vengeance.

Jim Ellington, with all the town tattlers, news-mongers, and busy-bodies, I leave to his own reward. I (though provoked beyond human endurance, and goaded beyond mortal forbearance with petty annoyances and galling insults, particularly bitter and wounding to my proud and sensitive soul, and warm, ardent, and passionate nature), am not altogether blameless myself. I was ever too impulsive and imprudent in my words and feelings. I never could be a fawning sycophant or hypocrite. Had I possessed the power of cool and calculating worldly deceit and selfishness, or been less open and frank in my nature I had not now been here. Long before my marriage, I knew of the hatred and opposition of my wife's relations to me, but fondly, vainly hoped that time, and so close and dear a tie would soften their feelings to kindness, if not to love, for Nannie's sake; and, for her sake, I should have borne more and longer than I did. I have been too hasty to resent the injuries and wrongs they heaped upon me; I have been too proud and sensitive, too unbending and unforgiving, too ready to resent and return an insult. By prudence and mildness, time and patience, I might have overcome their malice and hatred; but, alas! though easy to be led by kindness, I never could be driven. Nannie, though much to blame, was never intentionally so; young and inexperienced, she was too easily led and influenced by others, though her very errors were but proofs of her love and devotion for me. Of a warm and ardent temperament, she loved me with all the fervor of her true and guileless heart, with a depth and tenderness of affection, and an undying devotion that few, very few men are blest with on this earth, even in the best of wives. Forgive me, Nannie, oh! forgive me, if I have sometimes seemed careless and indifferent to your fond and tender caresses. If I have sometimes seemed cold and harsh in my words and manner toward you, when troubled and oppressed with the trials and cares of business; it sprang not from any want of love for you. Oh! I was ever ready to share all my joys with you, but hid my sorrows in my own bosom, that I might not give your gentle heart one useless pang. If I have not always *shown* and expressed that tenderness and affection which thy fond and yearning heart exacted and required (women ever cherish and remember the little tokens of love and regard more than we are aware of), believe me, it was not because I did not know and feel your worth and truth, or prized your affection. Ah! forgive me for any such *apparent* indifference. My heart was ever fond and true as yours, and I was proud of and happy in your love. Oh! Nannie, I have been too much blessed in the possession of you and your love, I fear, to be sufficiently grateful to Heaven for all my happiness. We never appreciate our greatest blessings as we should until they are taken from us. I never knew how happy I was in *you* and *your love*, or how much I loved you, until now when I am torn from the rich blessings of home, of wife and child, and all the fond endearments of mutual love and confidence. Oh! Nannie, my heart is wrung to think that you must suffer for my sake. May God grant to make you happy.

December 3, 1855.

FATE.

We are creatures of circumstances, though, to some extent, we are free agents, or *seem* so; yet, "there is a destiny which shapes our ends, rough hew them as we will." "*L'homme propose, et Dieu dispose.*" A thousand little circumstances over which we have no control, and of which we frequently have no knowledge, influence our actions and conduct, shape our thoughts and feelings, and affect our whole lives; thus forcing us to meet, make, and fulfill our destiny. I have always been, more or less, a fatalist; made such by the strange singularity and fatality of my own life I will only speak of a few instances of my past life, since I first came to Illinois; of my course and the *circumstances* that led to my present unfortunate position.

By an *accident*, very trifling in itself, I first was induced to come to Charlestown, Illinois. The morning after my arrival, before making myself known to my relatives, I repaired to the barber-shop, in company with a man named David Hamlin, whose acquaintance I then formed. While there, he exhibited to me a miniature of a young lady, his cousin, he said, which he had stolen from her, for mischief. I admired the picture very much, and remarked that I had seen the original, as the face looked very familiar to me; but when he told me her name was Nannie Ellington, I knew she was a stranger; yet, I warned him laughingly, that if she was his "sweetheart," I was destined, I thought, to marry her myself; that she was the first lady I had seen in Charleston, and if I was half so well pleased with the rest of the town, I certainly would make it my home for life.

One year from that time I had not met the original of the daguerreotype, and I was about to leave the State again forever, when an *accident* happened, which forced me to prolong my stay another year: I most strangely got into a difficulty with a man by the name of Allen, and became entangled so in the meshes of the *law*, that I was compelled to stay a year more than I had anticipated. By *accident* I met and was introduced to the original of the daguerreotype. I was much pleased with her, and she seemed so with me. She invited me to call and see her, which, for a long time I failed to do. She sent me word, repeatedly, that she would be pleased to have me call upon her. I finally went there, by *accident*, to a party. By *accident*, I went alone, and by *accident* I was left alone with her after the company had retired, and though with her but a few moments became aware that I loved her, and was beloved in return. By *accident* she first confessed her love, and I left her engaged to be married to her, and proud and happy of my good fortune. I met with many rivals, better known and wealthier and more fortunate in the good will of "the old folks," but, thanks be to the good faith and love of Nannie, I was the conqueror. We were married—but against the will of Nannie's mother, and of all the town-tattlers, and match-makers. But, in spite of them all, we lived happy, regardless of their envy and malice, until another *accident* occurred with some of our friends (my wife and my relations), which caused her mother to rage a-fresh against me; to abuse me, and endeavor to effect a separation between myself and Nannie. By a succession of *accidents* to aid her malice, she at length brought about an inveterate hatred of her husband, family, and friends against me, but without effect, upon my wife, at least, though they nearly drove her to madness and me to desperation. By an *accident*, James Ellington and Byrd Monroe quarreled, and drew me into it. By an *accident*, I met Ellington, and we spoke of his son's quarrel, and he being excited, abused and attacked me; when, in self-defense I shot him, from which he died. By *accidents and misconceptions* the whole affair was brought on, and, what seems stranger still, the night before the affair which resulted in Ellington's death, and my arrest and committal here, my wife dreamed that her father murdered me, and that he was dead himself; and I dreamed *three times*, that some one told me I was sleeping the last time with my wife; and several expressed fears that something sad would happen that day, so much so that I promised Nannie to be on my guard, and to stay at home that day, but, by *accident*, I was called away, and met with an *accident* which has up to this time, and *may* forever prevent my return.

These are a few of the *accidents* and circumstances which have produced all this past happiness and all this present misery. I have loved my wife as man seldom loves woman, and I have been blessed in her love beyond the common lot of man. We were very happy; we are now as miserable. Whether it may be permitted by fate for us to ever be happy again together, I know not. I can only hope for the best, and leave our cause in the hands of heaven.

December 3, 1855.

MY JEWELS.

I HAD a jewel—a rich and noble jewel—bright, brilliant, and beautiful, with a few slight spots upon its surface, which seemed but to increase rather than diminish its beauty and worth; and I loved it with a miser's love. It was the joy of my heart, the light of my life, and the pride of my soul. It was my beacon-star of hope and love. Day by day I wore it on my bosom, proud of its sweet luster and beauty, and blessed in its untold worth; and night by night I pressed it to my heart, and kissed it o'er and o'er again, blessed, beyond expression, in every mutual caress, and fond and tender glance of its soft, sweet, and love-lit eyes; while its rosy cheeks were suffused with the bright blushes of modesty and love, and its ripe, red lips were glued to mine in long and lingering kisses of rapture and bliss. Oh! I was never weary of loving and caressing my jewel, my own, my beautiful!

Upon its bosom there grew a pearl, a sweet and tiny gem; bright and lovely as angel's eyes, and I was wild with the thrilling excess of love, and joy, and happiness. Alas! I fear I worshiped them more than I did my God, for soon, oh! how soon, were they torn from me by the cruel, envious hands of FATE. By the stern decree of destiny, in one day, in one hour, I lost my all, my gem and jewel, my fortune and my liberty.

That jewel was my wife; that gem was my child! Oh! God, grant, in mercy grant, that they may once more be mine again.

December 5, 1855.

LIFE.

I SAW a youth wandering upon the shores of time; restless and weary he seemed, straying hither and thither, as if he sought to drown his soul's unrest in search of pleasure, or new and dangerous adventures. Sometimes he would suddenly start forward with rapid, hasty steps, as if in pursuit of a fair and fleeting form, which seemed fading forever in the dim distance far before him; then pausing again, he would look back upon the path he had just traveled, back upon the past as if in sorrow and regret; then turn, and with eager, anxious steps haste forward again, as if to catch the object of his vain pursuit, till wearied at length with disappointment and fatigue, he sank upon the earth, and gave vent to his sad complainings:

"Oh! why," he murmured, "are our hopes to be thus forever cheated? Why should man be thus forever doomed to pursue the false and fleeting form and airy phantom of happiness, which ever eludes his grasp? Oh! that some good spirit would but teach me how to secure this prize, and set my weary soul at rest!"

Immediately, as if at his invocation, three forms appeared. At his right hand stood a bright and glorious presence; at his left a dark and shadowy outline of an evil, shrinking form; in front an old man of venerable form and appearance. The latter gazed with pitying eye upon the restless, wearied youth, and thus addressed him:

"Alas! my friend, it is not ours to give what thou requirest. We can but place the means before thee. It is the province of these spirits on thine either side to make or mar. They are the guardians of thy fate, the angels of thy destiny. The angel upon thy right of such celestial light and heavenly form, is thy guardian angel, who is ever by thy side to appeal to thy better nature, and to whisper sweet words of hope and truth within thine ear, ever counseling thee to thine own good. Listen, oh! listen to that 'still, small voice.' 'T will lead thee to do good; and to do good is to be happy. That upon thine left, that dim, and dark, and shadowy form, is thy evil spirit, who appeals to thy passions, to thy impatient desires and imaginings. Oh! beware of the charms thou wilt meet in its siren voice and fatal power! Be wise, and learn, and know thyself. Be temperate and moderate in all things. Have forbearance and kindness for other's faults. Judge not partially. Consider thyself. Have 'Faith, and Hope, and Charity.' Govern thy passions. Love thy neighbor as thyself. Be slow to anger—slow to resent and punish—quick to forgive and forget, and thou wilt be happy and at length find that for which thou longeth, peace and rest. Peace is happiness, and rest is peace. The grave, too, is rest, but rest is also beyond the grave; beyond time and death—the boon of eternity."

When he had finished speaking, the old man's form vanished away into airy nothingness, and the seeker after happiness pursued his life-march, attended by his two angels.

Oh! how I longed to lay down my mortality and put on my immortality, and in the quietude of the grave forget my troubles and persecutions. When, oh! when shall my "weary spirit flee away and be at *rest?*"

How forcibly I can feel the Psalmist's wail: "I am sick at heart; my soul is weak; the flesh is strong, but now subdued." I am weary, weary of life and hope, of doubt and fear, and, oh! how I long for death.

A DARKER VIEW OF HUMAN NATURE.

NANNIE, my wife, has herself caused, in a great measure, the unfortunate event so lately enacted, and to a great extent has brought on all these misfortunes. She from the first time I ever met her, loved me—*loved me well and truly*, so much so that she first declared her passion; and this devotion and excess of love on her part first caused me to propose and resolve to make her mine. Willful and obstinate, warm and passionate, she braved her relatives' opposition, and loved me, I think, the better for it; met me often, and, finally, married me against their will. She was ever fond and tender in her love for me, and like all of her disposition, very exacting and requiring in the due and full return of her own warmth and tenderness. I was ever careless of outside show, and though I loved Nannie with all my heart and soul, I fear I never was, at least not always, as considerate and careful to show it, or to return her own quick advances and warm endearments, as I should have been. My heart reproves me, now, for not noticing or returning her tender words and fond caresses, with which she met me ever, even when absent only an hour. Often, when oppressed with business and care, and harassed by the malice of her own relations, I have went home to my meals unfit to notice or return the fondness of her welcome and the tenderness of her caresses; and though my heart was sensible of and grateful for all, yet, I fear, I often seemed to her fond exacting heart, indifferent and cold. Before my marriage I was a sad rake, courting and engaging myself to every girl I met. This Nannie knew, and, after I told her all my follies, I was too confident and secure in her love and devotion to me, and of my own power, to be strictly just to her and myself. I knew her love and confidence in me *so well*, that I fear I sometimes abused both. There was one of my amorous engagements (the last, I believe, before my marriage, and of which I fully informed her, before and after we were married), in which I now believe I did wrong. I allude to my engagement to ——. After I was married, for a long time, I foolishly kept up my flirtation with ——; and that, with my frequent carelessness, coldness and indifference to Nannie, now makes me feel that I wronged, grossly wronged and outraged her trust in me.

* * * * * *

She would willingly have sacrificed family, friends, and all the endearing and hallowed associations that lingered around her childhood's home, and been *more* than compensated—aye, perfectly happy in my love. But I was goaded to madness by the treatment and insults I ever and continually received at the hands of the Ellingtons, and, finally, give way to my long pent feelings of indignation—I began to return insult for insult. My poor Nannie, who had of late grown somewhat jealous and doubtful of my love, for which her sweet heart was always yearning and only required, was, by these doubts and yearnings, very uneasy and dissatisfied, and often complained to *them* of my apparent coldness and indifference, and often complained to *me* of the treatment she experienced from her family (only seeking to find if I truly loved her). Encouraged by these things, her mother became bolder in her abuse of me, and openly begged Nannie to leave me. She came to *my* house—quarreled with *my* mother—ordered *her*, my *mother*, out of *my own house*—and then came to *my* house again to beg Nannie to leave me; accusing me of having married Nannie for *her money;* that *she* (Mrs. Ellington) had never liked me; and that I was a spendthrift and a drunkard, and that if they ever gave me any thing I would spend it for whisky, etc.,—against all of which accusations my soul rose up in arms. I then ordered Mrs. Ellington and *my own mother* (oh! God, forgive me for that last!) never to come to *my* house again, unless they could come in peace and kindness toward Nannie and I. Satisfied I was is in the right, I resolved and swore *never* to receive any thing from my wife's parents, since they had charged me with such baseness, and publicly declared they never would give Nannie any thing unless she would leave me. I then refused to let Nannie visit them, thinking it best and not right that she would desire to visit a house where I was abused so much, and not welcomed to, even as a son-in-law, and maddened, too, to find that she did not resent their insults, as I thought she ought to do.

Ellington about this time, refused to pay for a set of china which they had presented to Nannie when we were first married, and sent and took away a cow which had been given her, and treated me and my mother very harshly. He was led to act thus, no doubt, by his wife, and the many tattlers who were striving to increase the flame. I had always liked Nannie's father, and loved him, too, for he was a good man, deserving of any one's love; but this last was too much, more than I could bear, and I became enraged, and made Nannie return all and every thing which they had given her; and then all was explained between us, and I verily believe we loved each other better, and were happier in each other's love, than if nothing had ever transpired to mar our peace. But, alas! this peace and happiness were not to last. Ellington, driven on by his unnatural wife, still pursued me, till the difficulty which ended in his death and my imprisonment occurred, for all of which Mrs. Ellington must one day answer before God! for, verily, but for her, and her hatred and insane abuse of me, all this sorrow had never been. I believe Ellington meant well, and would if left to himself, have done right; but, driven on by his wife and a thousand busy tattlers, he abused me—I resented—he attacked me—I defended myself, and his death and my incarceration were the consequences. Oh! let parents, by all these warnings and misfortunes, learn to use more charity and kindness toward their children, and never oppose, to such excess, their free and settled choice. How much, oh! how much misery have such family jars and disturbances brought on, when all might have been peace and happiness! But for this unjust hatred and abuse of me by Mrs. Ellington, Nannie and I would have been happy still, and Ellington alive.

After my arrest and commitment, and Ellington's death, Nannie was left without a home or protector. By her father's will she was disinherited unless she procured a divorce from me. She was not suffered to stay in her mother's house, except upon condition of never seeing me again. I was committed to jail, without bail, charged with murder, and the whole community excited against me, and nothing, apparently, to hope, but that I would be sent to the penitentiary. What could Nannie then do—alone, friendless, and helpless, as she was—with no home to go to? She was forced to accede to their wishes, and accept a home with them upon their own terms.

[In the following paper will be found Monroe's version of the killing of his father-in-law. The paper, as originally written, contains nothing valuable save what we have extracted. It is a letter to his wife, filled with requests, and expressions of endearment, and valuable only to her. He conceived it but a simple act of justice due to his wife that he should state the truth, the whole truth, and nothing but the truth to her, in regard to the killing of her father. It is needless to state that the *important* features in the case, as stated below, are fully corroborated by the evidence deduced at the trial in which he was convicted.—Editor.]

A STATEMENT OF FACTS.

In justice to myself, Nannie, as due to you, I feel called upon to narrate the true circumstances of this last sad affair. They are these:

On the night of the 18th of October, Byrd Monroe came to me very much excited (having already sent Howlett to me), and requested me to go with him, as he had just had a difficulty with James Ellington, in which he (James E.,) had said your father had given him (Byrd Monroe) and me the lie. I went with him, but in good humor. We did not find your father, but he and Jim quarreled again; in which I took no part, but laughed at them; only at the last I told Jim that if his father or any one else gave me the lie, I would then tell them they lied. We parted, and I came home and narrated to you all that occurred, as you will remember, and I also promised you I would not have a difficulty with any of them, if I could help it, unless I was attacked; and that I only asked, as I had ever done, to let me alone. The next morning I met your father accidentally in the street, and the affair of the night before was mentioned. I told him that I had nothing to do with it, and that I had been sent for and dragged into it, and that Jim had said that *he* had accused me of lying. He then gave me the lie, and offered to strike me with his cane. I drew back, and told him not to strike me. He then proposed and insisted that I should accompany him to Byrd Monroe's. I went with him to the store, but Byrd was not there. I then asked him why he should blame me for all that others said; that if, as he said, Byrd and John Monroe lied, let it be with *him and them*, and not blame me for all; that *I* had nothing to do with it—that I knew and cared nothing about it, nor did I see any good reason why I should be dragged into it. He then said I had told forty lies, to which I, of course, gave the lie. *He then struck me twice*, and choked me back upon the counter, when I shot at him, the ball just grazing the temple. He then threw me on the floor and jumped upon me, choking, beating and gouging me. I called upon the crowd to take him off. John Eastin called out, "D—n him, stamp him to death:" and he refused to be taken off, saying he wanted to kill me. What was I to do? I could not submit to be beaten to death, or have my eyes gouged out; and then, as my *dernier resort*, I fired again; which shot, alas! proved fatal. We were then separated, but too late. If John Eastin had not told him to kill me, and they had taken him off when I called upon them, all would have been well. But what else could I have done? He was a strong and powerful man; I was small and

A STATEMENT OF FACTS.

In justice to myself, Nannie, as due to you, I feel called upon to narrate the true circumstances of this last sad affair. They are these:

On the night of the 18th of October, Byrd Monroe came to me very much excited (having already sent Howlett to me), and requested me to go with him, as he had just had a difficulty with James Ellington, in which he (James E.,) had said your father had given him (Byrd Monroe) and me the lie. I went with him, but in good humor. We did not find your father, but he and Jim quarreled again; in which I took no part, but laughed at them; only at the last I told Jim that if his father or any one else gave me the lie, I would then tell them they lied. We parted, and I came home and narrated to you all that occurred, as you will remember, and I also promised you I would not have a difficulty with any of them, if I could help it, unless I was attacked; and that I only asked, as I had ever done, to let me alone. The next morning I met your father accidentally in the street, and the affair of the night before was mentioned. I told him that I had nothing to do with it, and that I had been sent for and dragged into it, and that Jim had said that *he* had accused me of lying. He then gave me the lie, and offered to strike me with his cane. I drew back, and told him not to strike me. He then proposed and insisted that I should accompany him to Byrd Monroe's. I went with him to the store, but Byrd was not there. I then asked him why he should blame me for all that others said; that if, as he said, Byrd and John Monroe lied, let it be with *him and them*, and not blame me for all; that *I* had nothing to do with it—that I knew and cared nothing about it, nor did I see any good reason why I should be dragged into it. He then said I had told forty lies, to which I, of course, gave the lie. *He then struck me twice*, and choked me back upon the counter, when I shot at him, the ball just grazing the temple. He then threw me on the floor and jumped upon me, choking, beating and gouging me. I called upon the crowd to take him off. John Eastin called out, "D—n him, stamp him to death:" and he refused to be taken off, saying he wanted to kill me. What was I to do? I could not submit to be beaten to death, or have my eyes gouged out; and then, as my *dernier resort*, I fired again; which shot, alas! proved fatal. We were then separated, but too late. If John Eastin had not told him to kill me, and they had taken him off when I called upon them, all would have been well. But what else could I have done? He was a strong and powerful man; I was small and weak in physical strength. I did not wish to hurt him, nor would I have harmed a hair of his head, *but to save myself.* I acted in self-defense to the last. I always liked your father, and thought him one of the best men in the world, until he was misguided and prejudiced against me, and abused and insulted me; and even then I did not censure him so much as I did others. It is not necessary for me to speak of what has previously passed. That you already know, and how much I had to bear; and if I *did do wrong,* 't was by returning defiance and contempt, insult and abuse, with prompt resentment. For *your* sake, I should have borne more; but who is perfect? As to the threats which I hear so much said about, I never made any more than you know, which was to defend myself if they attacked me, as I heard so often they intended to do. But I am here and can not help myself, and so, of course, many lies and much abuse will be heaped upon me.

A REQUEST.

Nannie, I am no religious bigot, no canting hypocrite. I despise, heartily despise the hollow, disgusting mummeries of all the reverend fools, and the whole sanctimonious crew. I despise them all—there's no religion in them; but, still, Nannie, I am, or *hope* I am, a Christian—my heart tells me I am. God does not require loud, open, public professions from the street corners and the house-tops, but daily, hourly love and worship, and pleasing to Him is the closet Christian. Long faces and prayers, hollow voices and sanctimonious airs, make up the sum of *worldly* religion. But the *true* Christian believes in his heart, and worships in silence, practicing 'Faith, Hope, and Charity.'

"Believe and you shall be saved." "Thou shalt be buried with me in baptism." "By the Holy Spirit and by water ye are born again."

My request is, Nannie, that you will be *baptised,* and that by *immersion.* I do not ask you to join any church—I do not care whether you do or not; nor, if you do, which one, so you will be *baptised,* for I know you *believe,* is all I ask. I hope we shall meet *again,* in a *better land.* But, at least, there's no promise to those who do not *believe,* and are not *baptised.* This is a simple request, Nannie, and it may be simple in me to make it: yet, I hope, you will do what I ask—*be baptised by immersion.*

Dolph.

LEAVING HOME.

A LEAF FROM A YOUNG MAN'S DAIRY.

ONE glorious evening, in November, 1851, I strolled away from the little town of ——, in the State of Kentucky. Passing through "Beech Grove," I spent an hour or more in tracing out the initials of the many names engraven upon the smooth bark of the majestic beech, seemingly of a century's growth, and towering to the skies. Oh! if you are a lover of nature, of the sublime and beautiful, go seek its shades and spend an hour in rambling there, and deem yourself a happy man if you should chance to meet with the fair maid of "Beech Grove." Passing thence and taking my way along the clear, silvery Licking, I soon found myself seated upon a knoll in the center of a fairy little isle, not far from town. 'T was that loveliest of all lovely seasons, Indian Summer; though somewhat sad and melancholy, I love it well. 'T is my favorite season. There is something so exquisitely sweet, so touchingly beautiful in it to me, like the sad sweet expression of sorrow upon the brow of youth, as if the spirit of summer was hovering over hill and dale and sighing o'er the stream and through the bowers, taking a last farewell of every tree and flower, and lingering long, as a bride lingers to take a last fond look at her many charms, ere she resigns them into the rude arms of the stern old winter.

The air was soft, warm and balmy—every gentle zephyr's breath that kissed my flushed cheek, or fanned my feverish brow, came laden with the fragrance of a thousand flowers. The golden eye of day was fast closing upon the scene; his last bright glance lay lingering upon the hill and stream in softened radiance. The sky was clear, save one snowy cloud, mirrored like an isle of light in the blue unfathomable depth of Heaven, touched and tipped by the rays of the setting sun, with crimson and gold, till it looked like some bright seraph's car.

All was calm and peaceful as an infant's dream; not a sound disturbed the sweet and soothing influence of the scene, but the warbling of the birds in the trees, and the low, soft murmuring of the stream as its waves rolled in silver brightness at my feet. Just at this time, I was aroused from my revery by that strange and indiscribable feeling of restless uneasiness, by which the mind, without the aid of any of the senses, becomes aware of the presence of another. Looking up, I observed a young man apparently some twenty-two or three years of age, walking slowly toward me, from the other extremity of the island. He was too deeply absorbed in his thoughts, apparently not of the most pleasant char acter, to perceive me. He advanced within a few feet of the knoll where I sat, and threw himself, with a deep sigh, at the foot of a large hawthorn tree.

Strangely interested in spite of myself, I remained still and motionless, gazing upon his sad pale face and dejected air; and thus became an unwilling listener to his meditations, which were uttered aloud in a sad and earnest tone of voice:

"Here, in this lone little isle, cut off as it were and shut out from the world, I seat myself again, and perhaps for the last time, at the foot of this tree, to recall many former visits here, with a lovely companion, who had an eye to see, a heart to feel and a mind to appreciate all the magic beauty of this lone little spot. Oft, at evening, have I wandered here with my book and flute, to enjoy the calm serenity of the scene, reading, musing and playing all my favorite airs, till wearied, I have laid them aside to listen to the more tuneful melody of nature's own sweet choir of feathered songsters in the grove; and soothed into forgetfulness of the world and all its cares, I have fallen asleep, while visions, sweet as ever visited our first parents in the garden of Eden, hovered over me.

"Here, the young and pleasure seeking folk of——— hold all their pleasant gatherings. Here, the first of May last, was assembled a joyous party of 'beautiful women and brave men,' and a fairer scene never met the eye or made the heart glad; there were music and dancing, strolling and promenading, while some were reclining in listless repose upon the velvet-like sward; there was the clear, ringing laugh of merry maidens, sweet as the echoes of a silver bugle; there was some flirting, a little coquetting, and much down right courting, done that day; there were whispering and blushing, ogling of eyes and squeezing of hands, all seasoned with the most delicate refreshments and generous wines. I never can forget that scene, so bright, so full of joy. If I should live on for ages, till the last day beams upon the world, 't would still recall some of the sweetest memories of life. But, oh! how changed is every thing here, now. The verdant bloom of spring has given place to the sear and faded leaf of autumn, that slowly, gently, and silently falls at my feet; so pass away the generations of the sons of men. Oh! where are all the green trees and the clustering vines, and fragrant, bright hued flowers—those beautiful beds of blue-bells, violets, cowslips and water-lilies, so lately springing up on every side, filling the air with their perfume, waving gracefully in the breeze, and bowing, as if in mock civility, to their own fair images reflected in the bright waters beneath? They are gone—all gone. Even the pure limpid stream that went rippling by so gaily, and laughing in the sun, seems sorrowing for its faded beauties, and goes moaning by as if in grief-weeping for the sunny month and sky of May. Sitting here and pondering on the joys of that bright scene, I imagine I can almost hear the sound of their busy, tramping feet, and the familiar tones of their merry voices, borne upon the gentle breeze, while I hold my breath and listen close, to catch the whispering tones, the low remark, and soft reply.

"Here we spread the feast, and here sat two youthful forms, whose young hearts had just awakened to the first soft touch of love; and here upon this bright spot, so thickly carpeted with grass and flowers, we danced away the rosy hours. Methinks I can see them now—those sylph-like forms gliding gracefully through the mazes of the dance. Here stood my dearest friend, besides his lovely partner, while, opposite, I stood by the side of her fair sister, just budding into womanhood, though still retaining all the sweet and artless grace and simplicity of the child—which like the opening bud, is sweeter far than the full blown rose. Here, with speaking eyes, glowing cheeks and heaving bosom, I first vainly tried to tell my love.

"But, why dwell upon the scenes? 'T is past, and never more, perchance, will I see another so bright, or mingle again with so many of the early friends of my youth. But a few short months have passed away since then, and they all are gone, while I sit here in sadness and alone, and the unavailing tears steel down my cheeks, all unheeded, and the wailing wind bears away each heaving sigh of grief. Ah! where are all of the fair forms and warm hearts and angel faces, that hallowed this spot, that day? They have all long since dispersed to their homes and avocations. Many a long and weary mile intervenes now, between hearts so closely united there in the bonds of friendship and love. Some have sought the busy haunts of the crowded metropolis—some are at the bar—some in the pulpit, and some, perchance, have sought, (as I am about to do) the distant West to build up a home in its wilds. This spot is sacred to me. It is hallowed by a thousand sweet associations of the past. Here I have wiled away many an hour in sweet converse and social intercourse with those I love. But alas! in a little while—a few hours at most—I must leave my boyhood's home and all these scenes so dear, to see them again, perchance, no more forever. May we all meet again, a happier company, midst brighter scenes, in a better world than this; and now, while pure thoughts and holy feelings come over me, let me kneel with full heart and streaming eyes, to pour out my soul in prayer."

* * * * * *

An hour later, I stood upon the thronged wharf where hundreds were assembled to see the mighty vessel cut her way through the trackless water. On she came like a thing of evil, belching forth

fire and smoke, leaving a glittering sheet of foam in her wake, and rounding-to with a shrill scream that would seem startle the spirit of the dead. Then, for the first time, I observed a group gathered around the same youth, whose meditations I had overheard; scores of old acquaintances and friends and youthful associates, were pressing eagerly forward to bid him farewell—while one, a tall graceful looking girl, apart from the rest, stood timidly back, with clenched hands, pale face and tearful eyes, gazing fondly upon him. Hastily bidding them all farewell, and brushing the tears from his eyes, he wrung his mother's hand, kissed her pale cheek, dashed down the steep bank and sprang aboard. Then, stationing himself upon the hurricane deck, he took a last fond look upon all his heart held dear—his boyhood home. With another shrill yell, warning all to get aboard, she glided swiftly away, and was soon lost to view behind a neighboring bend; bearing him on to his new home in the "far West," where we may, perchance, some time follow him in his future career. As the vessel passed out of sight, many a white handkerchief was waved from the shore, to that lone form, with many a heartfelt wish of kindness and sympathy; but the mother's eyes were raised to Heaven, and her lips moved as if in prayer; her eyes were tearless, but a deep and settled agony was stamped upon her pale and care-worn features. Slowly, with bent form and tottering steps, and lingering looks, she turned to seek what now must seem the deserted walks of home.

THOUGHTS OF DEATH.

"To think of summers yet to come,
That I am not to see;
To think of flowers yet to bloom
From dust that I shall be."

The above beautiful lines will express the feelings in which we all, more or less, indulge when contemplating our final end. Death—the common lot of all; none, great or small, high or low, rich or poor, but must sooner or later bow alike to thy dread scepter. Oh! Death! truly "in the midst of life, we are in death." Every breath brings us but nearer to the tomb, and proves, at the same time, the funeral knell of some departing spirit. After the few brief days of our short lives have passed away in turmoil and in strife, we turn away, sick at heart, to go and dwell in the silent city of death, and there find, beneath the sod, the rest we can not find on earth. Quietly do the eternal sleepers rest on their sepulchral couches. There is no strife, no vain distinctions there. The prince and peasant, master and slave, lie moldering together—generation after generaton is brought and laid by their side—the vain and pompous inscription on their monumental marble, tells of the centuries that have passed away; but the dead observe it not; all is unheard and unseen by them; the busy world of life goes on above them, but they hear it not; the sound of joy, or the sigh of grief, the voice of song, or the wail of despair, breaks not the solemn stillness which reigns in the silent city. The deep-toned bay of the watch-dog, the cannon's awful roar, or the thunder's rolling might,

"No more disturbs the deep repose,
Than summer evening's latest sigh
That shuts the rose."

Even now, while writing, the solemn knell of the tolling bell strikes mournfully upon my ear, and she, who was but yesterday the light and joy of the social circle in which she moved, and the home she made so blest and happy, is borne to her last resting-place.

Oh! in youth, when the heart beats high with hope and we are looking forward to the future with bright anticipations of joy and happiness, how unwelcome comes thy summons, oh, Death! yet 't is ever thus. The loveliest of our race the soonest pass away, and life seems but a waking dream—like the morning mist or the early dew, they pass from earth to Heaven.

In middle age, 't is yet the same. The spoiler comes and finds us, perchance, surrounded by a blooming family, in all the enjoyments of mutual love, and the endearments of connubial bliss, and whether he strikes ourself, the wife of our bosom or the cherub at her breast, the stroke is equally severe.

Even old age, dark and unlovely as it is, shrinks from death and would gladly stay yet a little while longer. We all dread to die—we all cling to life and shudder to think of thee, insatiate Grave! But oh! how dark and drear must be the gloom that overspreads the lost and hopeless sinner's soul, when death has summoned him hence and is about to depart on that long journey, to try the realities of the unknown future, to meet the Great Judge, face to face! All has failed him now. All that he has set his heart upon and clung to through life—alas! what are they now? What can wealth, and rank, and power, avail him? He sees, he he feels, that all is vanity. Oh! what would he not give to live his short life over again? How differently would he live it? The earth, the beautiful earth, with all its joys, all its blessings, is fast fading from his view. What are all his idols now? He must die and leave them. And oh! worse than all, he feels that he must stand condemned before the judgment-seat of an offended God! Oh! how he longs for *one* of his many misspent hours, in which he might repent—in which he might make a covenant of peace with Heaven!

How differently does the Christian die? How calm his look, how sweet his smile, while his spirit is passing away. To him the grave hath no terrors, death no sting; he knows that his Redeemer liveth, and that He will accompany him through the dark valley and shadow of death; that He will go with him into the narrow bounds of the cold and dreary tomb, to bring him forth again and clothe him in the bright and glorious robes of blissful immortality, and place upon his brow the crown of eternal life. How exultingly can the dying Christian sing, as he faces the dread "King of Terrors,"

"Oh, Grave! where is thy victory!
Oh, Death! where is thy sting?"

He knows that his body must die and be laid in the cold and silent tomb, to become food for worms; but he feels that his soul is immortal and can never die; and 't is he alone, who can truly say, "I do not fear to die."

As we, when weary with the toils and labors of the day, seek our chambers for repose, so will the Christian, when done with the sufferings of this world, welcome thee, oh, Death! and seek repose in thy last, long sleep. He will calmly fall into the Redeemer's arms, knowing that, in the morning of the resurrection, he will awake in His likeness.

Oh! who can doubt the immortality of the soul? Who after once raising his eyes aloft and contemplating the movements of those celestial worlds, can for an instant believe that man after a few short years of trial and trouble, shall be swept away, even as the brute creation, without one solitary trace remaining, as to who and what he was? Mind and matter differ widely in their elements, and man is the only animal endowed with mind. Even in sleep (that emblem of death), it is never at rest—but ever active. Of matter we can not destroy one particle, though we see it changing its form every day without surprise. Look at the silk-worm undergoing change after change, and passing from one stage of existence to another, until, at last, we see it a dark brown grub, apparently without life or motion; but lo! in a few days we behold coming forth from that loathsome object, a beautiful and bright-winged butterfly. See it spread its wing of azure and gold, soaring gracefully away upon the summer breeze; roving from flower to flower and basking in the warm sun light.

Oh! if God, from that dull worm, can bring forth a thing so beautiful, what shall the Christian be when he shall have burst the bars of death, arisen triumphant from the grave, with form divine, and put on celestial livery, to fly away on angel's wings to the bright and gorgeous courts of Heaven? How shall the Christian appear when arrayed in those shining robes, washed white in the blood of the Lamb, and mingle with that innumerable host congregated round the Throne of God? I sometimes feel as if I were tired of staying in this prison-house of clay, and long for angel-wings to "flee away and be at rest."

Oh! who would not be a Christian; who would not have the blessed hope and promise of life immortal beyond the tomb, eternal in the Heavens?

THE MAY PARTY.

On the first of May, 1851, the sun rose clear and bright; the sky was cloudless and every thing giving promise of a beautiful day, the young people of Falmouth indulged the brightest anticipations of a merry May day. But, alas! like many of the fondest hopes of youth, they were doomed to disappointment. The sky, hitherto so clear and bright, became suddenly overcast with black and heavy clouds, from whose dark bosoms came muttered thunder tones. A storm arose. Doubt, anxiety and gloom were now seen in the countenances lately so bright and joyous. The clouds soon passed away from the blue and laughing sky, but a heavy wind sprung up and increased in fury, until the stoutest trees, groaned and creaked and bowed their stately heads before the blast. So, by general consent, it was agreed to call the day 31st of April, and postpone the party till the morrow.

The ensuing morning was soft and balmy, and richly perfumed with the sweet odors of spring. The company, consisting of about twenty couple, were soon wending their way to the lovely little island, adjacent to the village, where all our parties of this kind were usually held. They soon arrived and gave themselves up to unrestrained mirth and glee.

It was a bright and lovely scene, and is engraven upon my heart with the magic pencil of memory too deep to fade while life shall last. Soon they broke up into groups—some feasting, some promenading, some romping and dancing and some sitting apart, were conversing in soft low strains. Conspicuous among the "love sick," was a long, lean doctor from Ohio, sitting close to and making himself particularly agreeable to his fair Dulcinia. They seem to be utterly unconscious that there were any other persons present and did nought but sigh and gaze into each other's eyes. As for myself, like the bee, I roved from flower to flower, sipping sweets from all, and romping and chatting with every one till the rosy hours flew away with the day, and evening came on.

I then fell into a fit of musing. The thought that the day, bright and beautiful as it had been, must soon close, and that all the light and happy hearts of that gay company must soon be separated, made my soul sad. While musing thus, sweet visions of the past came thronging quick upon me, but conspicuously shone the well-remembered scene that took place here one short year ago. Here, upon this spot, were there assembled most of the company now present.

Some that were here then, are missing now. She who was then the fairest of the fair and the gayest of the gay, is not here now. I miss that lovely form and angel face, and vainly listen to catch the sound of her sweet voice. Ah! never more its musical tones thrill the hearts of her mourning friends. She is gone—her voice is hushed in death. The places that knew her once and grew bright with her presence will know her no more forever. She is now an angel in Heaven. She is gone. Her short life has fled as some sweet dream, but her memory, like the music heard in other days, will long haunt and linger about the hearts of her friends. Her mourning sister—I miss her, too—like a drooping lily, is pining in sorrow at home.

From these sad reflections I roused myself, and sought the side of a fair but somewhat pensive nymph (whose eye grew brighter at my approach), and was soon deeply engrossed in reading, as in a book; every thought and feeling in it found utterance of her fresh and guileless heart. Here I sat until the company were preparing to go; we then reluctantly rose to leave. She told me she was going away from home, and would be absent for months, and that ere she departed, I must come and see her. Of course, I promised to do so. Taking her hand, I tenderly bade her farewell, promising to write her and entreating her not to forget me. Her eyes filled with tears, which I kissed away, endeavoring to soothe and comfort her. Looking up into my face with a languishing glance of love and desire, she pressed upon my finger a plain gold ring, with a wish and a sigh, a smile and a tear, and ere we parted, we had again and again exchanged vows of eternal love and constancy; vows to be forgotten in an hour, or only to be remembered with a smile.

THE VOYAGE OF LIFE.

AN ALLEGORY.

THIS was one of the scenes of my ever changeful dreams. In a fairy-like boat, so light was its construction, I floated swiftly but smoothly down a silvery stream. How I got there, I know not, as there are no way-stations in the railway land of dreams. I only know, that it was the fairest scene I ever beheld. On either side were green banks and far-stretching fields, whose verdure was interspersed and dotted with white cottages and shady groves; while here and there, creeping like silver serpents, little rivulets sparkled and glanced brightly in the sunlight. The bank, on either side, was strewn with sweet, gaudy and fragrant flowers, which ever and anon, I tried to pluck.

Methought my frail bark was oarless, so that I had no power to check or guide its course. But little recked I of that. As I glided down the stream, and onward, and still onward, I cast a delighted eye on all around me. The banks were carpeted with flowers, while the sweet melody of innumerable birds and bees greeted my ravished senses, as it poured in one continuous music-stream from the green woods. I uttered an involuntary exclamation of delight, which was quickly changed to one of affright, when I discovered the form of a decrepid old man rise up in the far end of my boat. In faltering accents I demanded of him who and what he was.

"If you were wise," said he, "you would already have known me."

His tones were so harsh and discordant, that I shuddered in every nerve. At length, I ventured to ask him how he came there, and requested him to leave my boat, as his presence was disagreeable to me. As to leaving the boat, he refused, saying:

"Even were I so disposed, I could not do it, for the river of life admits of no stopping. When once you have embarked upon its waters, you must sail to your destined port and tarry not."

"But," said I, "this boat is not yours, and I wish not your company."

"True, sir," replied my strange companion; "the boat is not mine; yet am I the one appointed by faith to pilot all who voyage to the ocean of eternity. When once you reach the shore unseen by mortal eye, then, and then only, can I leave you to return and pilot others, as I do you. Such is my duty and such has been my constant labor since the beautiful earth first sprang from chaos; and such will be my task until time shall be no more."

I now gave myself up in despair and gazed in silence upon the beautiful scene around me. At length, rendered desperate, I turned to the grim old pilot, and ultimately threatened and expostulated and exhorted him to hasten on to the end of the dismal journey. He coldly bade me be quiet.

"Foolish boy," said he, "if I could comply with your threats, your prayers and your expostulations, and put leagues that are now far ahead, in our rear, you would but be the nearer to yon dismal port," pointing with his long and bony finger to a frightful gulf roaring in the dim distance and whose solemn sound now for the first time reached my ears. In fear and trembling, I drew closer to the strange old man.

"And must my boat enter that dismal gulf?" I cried.

"That whirling vortex, is death," was the answer.

Then I prayed him to stop, but he laughed at my entreaties.

"Be wise, foolish mortal," said he, "and treasure up my words; improve your opportunity, and I will be your friend. Look again on that sea of death. To the left, see that black and yawning gulf, and listen to the hideous groans and screams that issue from its awful depth;—*that is the gulf of the damned*, and *there*, shall surely perish all who fail to make me their friend. Now cast your eyes to the right. See that calm and placid lake, teeming with bright and beautiful islands, from which comes such heavenly melody—such sweet songs of praise—*that*, is called *the haven of rest*—the harbor of the ransomed. Be wise, listen to me, and I will pilot thee there."

I seized his hand, and with tearful eyes and quivering lips, thanked him for his good counsel, and vowed to him eternal devotion. He smiled and laid his hand upon my head so gently, that, as I looked up into his hitherto repulsive face, I thought he had more than earthly beauty.

"Wondrous man," I exclaimed, "tell me who and what thou art."

"I am one feared and hated by all mankind; represented as a fell destroyer, wielding a scythe and mowing down the race of men. My name is Time. But I am the *friend* of man, and yet, he will not know it. I soothe his sorrows and mitigate his severest vows. If thou wilt, I will be thy friend also. I am the friend of all who are good and wise."

"Then," said I, "be the friend, also, of my mother and my sister."

"Thy mother," he replied, "has long known me. We are already friends. Thy sister, too, shall know me better, soon. Look," and gazing in the direction he pointed out, I beheld my sister in another tiny bark, gliding down the rapid-rolling river, and gayly plucking the flowers that laved their blushing cheeks in the silver stream. Her merry laugh was echoing musically from shore to shore, and, in her happiness, she seemed unconscious of the presence of her grim old pilot, Time. Near her was a childish form, playing carelessly with the rippling wâves.

"Now look again"—I looked, and far down the fast widening stream, beheld gliding tranquilly along, the boat bearing my mother. Methought, ever and anon, she would gaze through the dim distance till her eyes would rest upon our tiny bark, beckoning us on, with smiles and tears, to join her; and then she would turn again and gaze far down the stream, through clouds of mist, upon the vast expanse of the future.

Memory ran back through all the days of my childhood, dwelling here and there, upon some act of disobedience to thee, oh! my mother; and I silently vowed, for thy sake, to sin no more "against heaven and in thy sight," but to make friends with the old man, Time, and sail to that "haven of rest," to join thee there, forever.

My dream was ended.

MY MOTHER.

I love my neighbor, love my friend,
  And my Masonic brother;
I love all who will right defend,
  But more, I love my Mother.

I love my fair fame far before
  All things on earth together;
I love my own just right, but more
  Than life, I love my Mother.

I have a sister good and kind—
  With life I would defend her,
But love my mother more refined,
  And still more strong and tender.

I have a little orphan niece,
  I love her like a father;
But, oh! I will, till life shall cease,
  Still love thee best, my Mother.

I know a little maiden fair,
  Of fairy form and feature;
Of guileless heart and beauty rare—
  I love the little creature.

She 's gentle, good and true, I know,
  I lov'd when first I met her;
I love her passing well—but, oh!
  I love my Mother better.

Whene'er I wander far and wide,
  From one land to another,
Then, more than all the world beside,
  I think of thee, my Mother.

When towards home in haste I hie,
  I know there is no other
That will so patient watch and fly
  To meet me, as my Mother.

When happy-hearted, light and free,
  There 's not on earth another
That can so sympathize, or see
  The good that 's in me, Mother.

When sorrow clouds my brow with care,
  And all the world together,
Look coldly on, oh! who shall dare
  To love me as my Mother?

And when in danger, doubt and dread,
  And troubles darkly gather,
Whose heart has e'er so quickly bled
  For me, as thine, my Mother?

And when the world's cold selfishness,
  My best afflictions smother,
I come to thee, in my distress,
  To counsel me, my Mother.

Oh! Mother, oft I 've made thee feel
  Full many a pang distressing,
But thou didst quick forgive and kneel
  To ask for me a blessing.

I was a wild and wayward child,
  And oft was found transgressing,
But, Mother, thou wast ever mild,
  And gentle and caressing.

Oh! Mother, thou wast early left
  A widow, poor and lonely,
With none to help, though sore bereft,
  With God to look to, only.

And those who should have been thy stay,
  Would no assistance render,
But planned how they might take away
  Thy means, though they were slender.

Thou couldst have had, at thy command,
  Those friends of widowed mothers,
That great, and good, and glorious band,
  My father's Mason brothers.

But thy proud heart could never ask
  From all the world a penny,
But, bravely took thee to thy task,
  Depending not on any.

For twenty years, since Father 's gone,
  Of suffering and of sorrow,
Thou bravely toiled, still hoping on
  For better things to-morrow.

With aching heart, and failing sight,
And fingers sore and bleeding,
Thou hast toiled on, both day and night,
Thy orphan children feeding.

But, Mother, God has heard thy prayer,
To thee a son He 's given,
Who 'll nourish thee with tender care,
'Till thou 'lt go home to Heaven.

And, Mother, now I 've grown to be
A man, both strong and willing,
I 'll work for thee, and comfort thee,
While I can earn a shilling.

Ah! Mother, thou art growing old,
Thy feeble frame 's fast failing,
Thy hands are thin, thy limbs are cold,
And thou art ever ailing.

Thine eyes are dim, thy hair is gray,
And death is o'er thee creeping;
But when thou 'rt gone, I 'll come and lay
Me down where thou art sleeping.

Oh! Mother, soon thou 'lt go from me—
Would we could go together!
But, though we part, I 'll come to thee
Again, in heaven, Mother.

Say, Mother, who shall then advise
Thy son, with truth and feeling;
Still, thou wilt whisper from the skies,
"Be faithful, and believing."

Dear Mother, when we meet up there,
Say, shall we know each other?
Ah! yes, my joy you first will share,
You 'll first receive me, Mother!

Oh! there I will my Father meet,
My Sister, and my Brother;
Then, Mother, there, in union sweet,
We 'll all praise God together!

"I 'M WEARY OF THIS LIFE."

I'M weary, weary of this life—of all this senseless round,
Of this vain search for happiness, for pleasures never found;
Of silly pride of place and power, and this cold world's mistrust,
This groveling strife for worldly wealth and things of earthly lust.

I 'm weary of this dull routine—this daily round of care,
Of this vain toil, this petty strife, for gold and silver ware;
Of hollow hearts, and shallow brains, and would-be Christians, too,
Of reverend hypocrites, and all the sanctimonious crew.

I 'm weary of all human joys,—of human hopes and fears;
Of every source of happiness, of the ebb and flow of years;
Of all this yearning soul's unrest, this "prison-house of clay,"
This crumbling frame of earth and air, its slow but sure decay.

But soon this heart shall cease to beat, this fount of tears be dry,
And this immortal soul shall *test* its aspirations high;
My yearning spirit then may find, freed from this aching breast,
Its destined paradise of love, its happy home of rest.

Then with some kindred spirit sweet, I 'll roam in bowers above,
Where all is joy, unending bliss, and sympathy and love;
Where days and years, and hopes and fears, no more shall ever be,
But youth shall last, and know no past, through all eternity.

LITTLE THINGS.

How few observe, or even dream,
  What little things may bring about;
We seldom are just what we seem,
  And few know how to draw us out.
In us, each day, great change is wrought,
  We never are two days the same;
Each day brings some new scheme, or thought,
  To change our object, end, and aim.

I was once, in heart, a very child,
  But manhood's cares oppress me now;
Maturer years have made me mild,
  And left their record on my brow.
'T was little things that changed my heart,
  And made me cold, and stern, and calm;
And little things but gave the start
  To all that 's made me what I am.

I know men's minds, amd seldom fail
  To ken them like an open scroll;
I listen to each flattering tale,
  But read aright the secret soul.
And gentler woman's softer heart,
  I read it in her soul-bright eye;
The conscious blush—the sudden start,
  Betrays the most reserved and shy.

Of smallest parts our life 's made up,
  And parts but form a perfect whole;
Of little drops, the bitterest cup
  Is filled, that stirs the human soul.

And love, with winning ways and wiles,
  The saddest human heart can bless;
And gentle words, and kindly smiles,
  Make up the sum of happiness.

I sometimes gay and cheerful seem,
  And smile as once I smiled of yore;
Ere childish joys, and boyhood's dreams,
  Had fled, alas! forevermore.
When nature weeps, the bow is born,
  Of hope and promise in the skies,
So a mother's care, in youth's bright morn,
  Taught faith and hope, that never dies.

Soft, murmuring streams, among the hills,
  That, sparkling, leap the pebbles o'er;
And tiny rills, the ocean fills,
  And swells Niagara's awful roar.
From little things the comet springs,
  To burn and blaze through endless years;
His song at eve the emmet sings,
  To swell the music of the spheres.

TO MY CIGAR.

I LOVE to sit for hours alone,
  And muse o'er my cigar,
Of happy hours I once have known
  With early friends afar;
Of childhood's scenes, and youth's sweet dreams,
  That still my heart holds dear,
Till the present, past, and future seems
  To blend in one soft tear.

I love the "weed," the grateful "weed,"
  It soothes my troubled mind;
'Tis an ever ready "friend in need,"
  A friend both true and kind.
Its fragrance sweet, when sad, I sip
  To "drown dull care" awhile;
'Tis sweeter far than woman's lip,
  More constant than her smile.

I love to watch the circling rings,
  As round they wheel and play;
Bright images, like angels' wings,
  Float gracefully away;
Unnumbered forms of air and light,
  I see with half closed eyes;
And strange, fantastic figures bright,
  Like mimic rainbows rise.

Each fragrant puff my spirit warms,
  And elevates my muse;
Each gentle breath and taste hath charms
  To chase away the "blues."
Let learned doctors rail and rant,
  Their bills (pills) are under par,
While I 've the "tin," despite their "cant,"
  I 'll smoke a good cigar.

SOME THINGS I LOVE.

I LOVE a man with an independent soul,
Who reasons, thinks, and proudly spurns control;
With a proud, high heart—that brooks no wrong,
No insult, from the overbearing strong;
But will, if rightly asked, forgive the wrong,
Try to forget, and strive to get along.
  I love a woman, with a woman's heart,
Unsullied by the base, deceitful art
Of coquette, or of flirt, but true and kind,
For such is woman's nature, when refined.
  I love a maid, with maiden modesty,
And artless grace, and sweet simplicity;
Those pure and guileless hearts, an open scroll
Of love, and truth, and constancy of soul.
  I love a friend with an open heart and hand,
With an open eye, and speech of fair demand;
That 's ever ready, quick, and bold of heart,
When I 'm not by, to bravely take my part;
That loves me for myself, and not for gold;
Who would be true, though all the world were cold;
True to his friend, true to his own true love,
True to himself, and true to God above.

LINES

TO A YOUNG LADY ON THE DEATH OF HER SISTER.

SCARCE eighteen summers yet had flown
  Away in joy and mirth,
Scarce eighteen winters yet had blown
  The roses from the earth;
When thy sweet sister, like a rose,
  Fell blasted in full bloom,
Her weary spirit sought repose,
  And found it in the tomb.

She was a mild and gentle child,
  And kind and dutiful,
She was as fair as angels are,
  And good as beautiful;
She was too fair, and pure, and bright,
  To linger longer here;
The sweetest flowers soonest fade
  In this terrestrial sphere.

Though sickness, sorrow, pain and death,
  Are found in every clime,
They can but blast our bloom and breath,
  They can but shorten time;
We should not fear, nor from them flee,
  They 're angels in disguise,
And sooner, o'er life's troubled sea,
  They waft us to the skies.

Amid a band, a glorious band,
  Before God's throne of light,
Thy angel sister now doth stand
  Most beautiful and bright;
With unseen hand she beckons thee
  To join that glorious throng,
Whose golden harps ring loud and free,
  In sweet celestial song.

The memory of her virtues may
  Still guide thy steps aright,
For unseen angels 'round thy way
  Are hovering day and night;
And her immortal spirit now,
  From sin and sorrow free,
Doth unto God with angels bow.
  To intercede for thee.

Then weep not, wail not, though she 's gone
  That from thy side she 's riven,
For fast the day is rolling on,
  When you may meet in heaven.
Remember what her last words were:
  "I do not fear to die;
I 'm going home—oh! meet me there;
  Meet me beyond the sky!

"I am prepared—I want to go—
  I know I am forgiven—
Oh! do not weep—it must be so—
  We 'll meet again in Heaven!"
Then weep no more, shed not a tear,
  But trust the word God 's given;
Embrace his cause, the way is clear,
  You shall meet her in Heaven.

THE HAWTHORN.

At the close of the evening, as twilight came down,
I strolled to the grove at the east of the town;
And along a lone path, with a lingering tread,
I strayed, sadly musing on joys that had fled.

'Neath the bright waving boughs of an old hawthorn,
That were blooming so gayly, one beautiful morn,
I sat on the trunk of a moss-covered tree,
And a maid of sixteen was sitting by me.

But the scene was now changed to darkness and gloom,
Its beauties all faded, its brightness and bloom,
As I sat on the trunk of that same old tree,
For the sweet girl no longer was sitting by me.

The leaves were all fallen, and desolate the scene,
Where I wandered that morn with the maid of sixteen;
But the bare, naked boughs, so dear to my heart,
Were watered with tears ere I rose to depart.

"TO ADA."

You bid me forget thee, you say that all 's over,
  That you must no longer remember the past;
You tell me to meet thee no more as a lover,
  That the sweet spell is broken, is ended at last.

"I wish not to remember," then *go*, and forget
  The bright, glowing schemes of the future we planned;
When I kissed away fondly the sweet tears that wet,
  Thy cheek, when you pledged me your heart and your hand.

Yes, *go*, and *forget me*, I 'll never complain,
  Whatever of sorrow my soul may endure,
I 'll bear it in silence; but never again,
  Will I trust in the faith that any are pure.

I 'll never forget *thee*, 'tis all a vain task,
  To stifle the feelings I 've cherished so long;
I can not forget thee, my *love* I may mask,
  But my *heart* can ne'er sing another new song.

There 's a charm in thy name, a holy, sweet spell
  'Round the innermost chords of my sad heart entwined,
And though I must bid thee a final farewell,
  Thy image, in memory, 's forever enshrined.

I 'll think of thee ever, wherever I go,
  Through each scene of life, in sadness or mirth;
I 'll think of thee ever, in weal or in woe,
  As the brightest, the purest, the dearest on earth.

Farewell, then, though dear one, may God ever bless
  Thy heart with true friends, who 'll never deceive;
May the angels of love, with a gentle caress,
  And a sweet smile of welcome, thy spirit receive.

MY FLUTE.

I love thee well! dear, good old flute,
  I love each soft and gentle tone;
To me thy lips are never mute,
  With thee I never am alone.

Thy gentle voice, when I am sad,
  Awakes, inspires my languid muse;
And my proud heart, when I am glad,
  It soothes, and softens, and subdues.

Thy thrilling tones, so wildly clear,
  So sadly sweet, go where I will
In this wide world, I seem to hear
  Their echo sounding near me still.

To thee I freely speak each thought—
  A confidant of thee I 've made;
And thou art true, for ne'er in aught,
  Hast thou my confidence betrayed.

I know thy worth, I 've tried thy truth,
  For many long and weary years,
From that sweet, sunny season, youth—
  That April day of smiles and tears.

Companion, relic, friend, and part
  Of happy days, that 's gone before;
From boyhood thou hast cheered my heart
  With loving, sweet, and holy love.

Of all my early dreams and hopes,
  The sweetest memories are thine;
I 'll cling to thee 'till heaven opes,
  Her golden gates to me and mine.

I 've other friends, whose love I prize
  As life itself, for friends are few;
But none so free from all disguise,
  And none so constant, none so true.

A battle with the world, whose cold,
  And hard, and hollow hearts I hate;
I smile to see them sell for gold,
  Their hopes of heaven, and call it "*fate!*"

I mingle with the young and gay,
  In pleasure's bright and brilliant train,
But soon I sadly turn away
  To pour my soul in some wild strain.

I feel that each sweet song of thine
  Has been to me in mercy given,
My thoughts and feelings to refine,
  And lead my spirit up to heaven.

Like some bewildered, shipwrecked tar,
  Whose hopes and prayers are all to see
His "friend and guide," the Polar Star,
  So ever turns my heart to thee.

Let others sneer, in cold disdain,
  I'll speak in praise of thee, old friend,
And seek thee still, in joy or pain,
  When I've an idle hour to spend.

And oh! with faith, and hope, and love,
  As day by day I'm toiling on,
Thy songs shall waft my prayers above,
  Where many, that I've loved, are gone.

In thy sweet voice I seem to hear
  Familiar tones from "spirit land;"
As if the "loved and lost" were near,
  With many an unseen angel band.

On rushing pinions, pure and white,
  My angel father seems to come,
With kindred angels, flashing bright,
  To bear my weary spirit home.

TO "BAT"—A FAREWELL.

Farewell, fair friend! a long farewell,
  From thee I sadly sever;
The words to me come like a knell,—
  I feel we part forever.

Farewell! if we should never meet
  Again, thy memory will,
Like some sad strain of music sweet,
  Long haunt my spirit still.

Oh! each pure thought of thee has wrought,
A spell about thy name;
Thy soaring soul my spirit taught,
A higher, nobler aim.

Why should the heart thus yearn to know
A being pure and good?
We seldom meet them here below,
Nor prize them as we should.

A yearning deep for the good and fair,
To every soul is given;
All pure and holy feelings are
As beacon lights to heaven.

I prized thee, aye, as all must do,
Who reverence truth and worth;
I 've ever loved the good and true,
The bright and pure of earth.

I loved thee as a star that shed,
Its soft, sweet light on all;
But youth's sweet dreams of love have fled,
As leaves in autumn fall.

Farewell! may angels guard and guide
Thee through the ills of Time!
We 'll meet again, though severed wide,
In a brighter, better clime.

That clime where 'tis forever spring,
Where flowers immortal bloom,
Where every wandering zephyr's wing
Comes laden with perfume:

Where seraphs strike their harps of gold,
And angel voices blend;
Where all are young, where none grow old,
And life shall never end.

TO ONE WHO WILL UNDERSTAND IT.

Affections bloom and blossom bright,
But if, in blooming, blast,
They shrink beneath the bitter blight,
And, withering, die at last.

Those early, fresh, and fragrant flowers
Of love, are sweet and pure;
Too pure for this cold world of ours,
They seldom long endure.

Their fragrance fleet our senses greet,
To pass away with tears;
We 'll never meet with aught so sweet,
In all our after years.

You might have won my hand and heart,
If we had sooner met;
But on love's stage I 've played my part,
A part I 'll ne'er forget.

I might have loved thee well and truly,
As any one on earth;
I do respect thee much, and duly
Appreciate thy worth.

I 'll ever love thee as a sister—
May this thy heart console,
There 's ne'er a Miss but there 's a Mr.,
To own her soft control.

Forgive my fun, no wrong I 've done,
'Tis all I ask of thee,
By yonder sun, I 'm not the one
To bow or bend the knee.

Of bachelors there 's lots and scores,
A plenty and to spare,
Who 'll kneel to thee, upon "all-fours,"
To swear that thou art fair.

Long ere we had been thrown together,
I had no heart to give;
Long since I learned to love another,
And must love while I live.

A maiden lovely, young, and fair,
And graceful as a fairy,
With none but her I 'll fortune share.
And none but her I 'll marry.

Her brow is like a throne of light,
Where truth her glory twines,
Her soulful eye, a window bright,
Through which her spirit shines.

A gentle, guileless, girlish creature,
Half woman and half child,
And soul and sense, in every feature,
Are beaming soft and mild.

A gentle, guileless, girlish creature,
Though long from her exiled,
I 've sacred held each cherished feature,
Since first on me she smiled.

I 'll ne'er forget her, though I rove
  On every land and sea;
Her sweet, confiding love and trust
  Are dearer still to me.

Oh! love 's a living, lasting flame,
  And gilds our sorrows o'er;
To memory each beloved name
  Is hallowed evermore.

When once the heart hath learn'd to sing
  Love's sweet and holy song,
Its music thrills each chord and string,
  And vibrates late and long.

LINES

WRITTEN AND PRESENTED TO MY SISTER UPON HER WEDDING DAY, WITH A COPY OF THE BIBLE.

SISTER, this book I give to thee,
  Upon thy wedding day,
That it may speak to thee for me,
  When I am far away.
This day, my sister, seals thy fate,
  For weal or woe through life—
Unites thee to thy chosen mate—
  Makes thee his wedded wife.

This day you give your heart and hand
  To him who won your love—
Oh! may that union sacred stand
  Till you both meet above!
Thy choice, my sister, I approve,
  And welcome my new brother;
He is my friend—a friend I love—
  Long we 've been friends together.

He has a proud and manly heart,
  A high and noble soul;
With love and truth he 'll do his part,
  But will not brook control;
Then, sister, let no harsh word mar
  Thy peace and quietness;
Nor ever let a useless jar
  Disturb thy happiness.

In future, strive to please him well,
  As you would strive this day,
Remember, that you 've said, "I will
  Love, honor, and obey."

And when his heart is bowed with care,
  And trials press him sore,
Then, sister, then 'tis thine to share
  His heart forevermore.

Oh! ever meet his coming feet
  With welcome kind and true,
His presence greet, with smiles as sweet
  As love would have thee do.
Oh! with kind words of love and grace,
  And sympathizing eyes,
The world will prove a pleasant place,
  And home a paradise.

Oh! sister, read this book with care,
  With patient mind and heart,
And read it with the constant prayer
  For aid to do thy part.
Sister, may God in mercy bless
  Thy union, while you live,
And may both find that happiness
  That He, alone, can give.

And may you both in wisdom's ways,
  And in the paths of peace,
Delight to walk through all thy days,
  And all thy joys increase;
And, oh! when death dissolves the tie
  You form this day, of love,
Oh! may you then, beyond the sky,
  Be joined again above:

Be joined where 'tis forever spring,
  Where flowers immortal bloom,
Where every breeze or zephyr's wing
  Is laden with perfume;
Where seraphs strike their harps of gold,
  And angel voices blend—
Where all is youth—where none grow old—
  Where life shall never end.

TO THE PUBLIC.

FALMOUTH, *December* 6, 1856.

IN presenting the following pages, I feel it to be an imperative duty I owe to the memory of him whose narrative you have before you, as well as for the sake of the truth, to notice some of the causes that led to the untimely end of Mr. Ellington; also the illegal and unjust proceedings that marked the whole of Monroe's confinement, trial and end. In doing so, I shall not attempt to give the whole in detail, but shall confine myself to some of the leading causes.

The family difficulty doubtless originated out of the opposition of Mrs. Ellington to the marriage of her daughter with Monroe. She was opposed to the marriage from the commencement of Monroe's visiting the house, and even after the ceremony incessantly poured forth her invectives against her son-in-law's frequently visiting the house; and unmindful of her duty as a mother, who should have had the interest of her children at heart, did much to break up the harmony that existed between Monroe and his wife; thus the difficulty originated, aided by the newsmongers of the town—those busybodies who, never having any business of their own must necessarily attend to others: such characters may be found in almost every village.

For a long time Ellington and Monroe were as they should have remained, friends; but alas, they remained not so; reports of an aggravated character were whispered to Monroe purporting to come from Ellington, and vice versa; but those characters already alluded to, uniting in their exertions, finally succeeded in breaking off the friendship and establishing a feeling of dislike between them; and doubtless caused both to say many things against each other that otherwise never would have been said or thought. It may be proper here to say, that Mr. Ellington was a man of social feelings, quiet and hard to excite to anger, but firm and resolute. Monroe, though social in his feelings, was of an excitable disposition, apt to speak free, and quick to resent an insult.

I regard both Ellington and Monroe as the victims of circumstances, rather than censure; but from the day upon which the fatal trigger was pulled, the whole community, without inquiring whether there were any palliating circumstances attending the fatal act, seemed determined to have Monroe's life whether right or wrong. Thus the harmony that existed between those men was destroyed, and consequently they frequently met with thoughts not of peace in their hearts; but after conversing, would find that the reports were not true and without a shadow of foundation, and then they would part in peace.

Ellington was a man of long standing in the county, and had perhaps as many friends as any one in the county; and I doubt not, justly so; for, from what I know of him he merited the esteem of all. He was a man of considerable wealth, which perhaps added to his popularity as a man; whereas Monroe was, comparatively speaking, a stranger, having not yet been in the place quite four years; not able to command but small means, and could consequently call but few his *friends,* and most of those afterward seemed to desert him, leaving him in the hands of Ellington's friends, and his enemies. Whether those friends were prompted thus to forsake him for fear of a personal attack, or for fear of endangering their property, or for fear that they should be called upon to aid him with their means, yet remains to me unknown; but doubtless they were afraid of both. Those few friends who seemed to stick to him and do all they could for him, did not consider it safe to openly defend or speak in his behalf.

I shall not attempt to give a history of the trial, but merely give a few facts connected therewith. I have always considered it a mockery—a mere show or pretense of dispensing justice. During the whole course of the trial, the court-room was crowded to overflowing, so much so that it was impossible to keep order; scoffs and jeers might be seen and heard throughout the entire crowd. While the lawyer for the defense was making his speech, he was frequently interrupted by the murmurs, or rather, decided efforts of the friends, or rather, of their hired or excited multitude. By these means the jury was intimated, or even I might say, it was overawed by the mob, and were compelled even in self-defense to return the verdict they did.

The judge, for not adjourning the court, owing to the threatening of the mob, is reprehensible, when it was evident to every impartial mind, that a fair trial, under the excitement, could not be had; such even as the law, in its most strict construction, guarantees to every one, but should be extended to all, let their crimes be ever so great or aggravated. During the trial, the rope was in the court-room and even held up before the eyes of the court and the prisoner, by some of the mob, without the judge or the sheriff daring to reprimand them; and a guard for the prisoner was not even allowed, but he was suffered to be pressed upon and howled after by fiends wearing the human shape ; showing thereby the determination of the populace, and deterring the friends of law and order from taking the course that humanity and justice required at their hands. The sheriff, John R. Jeffrees, of Coles county, appears to have taken particular pains to court the favor of the mob populace, using all means to render the prisoner's life, while yet on earth, miserable—if possible more so than it was; as if giving him a foretaste of *the hell* which they thought he should enjoy, withholding from him as far as possible the comfort of hearing from, or seeing his friends.

He was placed in a dark, cold and dreary cell, not allowed fire by the court, and not until he had suffered much, were his friends permitted to add a little to his comfort by placing a stove in his cell and placing fuel at his disposal. The Governor, by representations of a few of his friends, suggested to the *aforesaid* sheriff of Coles county the propriety of the removal of the prisoner to some adjoining county or the summoning of a sufficient guard to defend him in his duty and to protect the prisoner's life. He did neither; though frequently appealed to by myself and other friends of Monroe, he said he had a sufficient guard to protect the prisoner, and would do it. But alas, on the day, where were the *stanch* guard and *the sheriff?* They were not to be found; no defense made; no effort made to save the unfortunate from the infuriated and highly excited crowd. Thus stands John R. Jeffrees, sheriff of Coles county, on whose head, perhaps, more than on any other, rests the fate of Monroe.

James Cunningham, the brother-in-law of Mr. Ellington, said to be the wealthiest man in the county, to make his words good, as I frequently heard, *i. e.* that Monroe should be hung law or no law, or he would spend every dollar he was worth, rode night and day to collect his more than fiends in human shape to accomplish his aim.

I shall only notice some few of those more particularly engaged in the diabolical deed. One by the name of Fleming, acted as hangman on the occasion, though since he has been heard to say, "he would never have engaged in the like, had it not been for others." The leaders not having courage to step boldly forward, and do their dirty work, pushed others forward. One of these, O. B. Ficklin, even pushed Fleming forward, when he would have backed out, and compelled him to complete the dastardly outrage. James D. Ellington, I should pass by unnoticed, did not justice to the dead as well as to place the living in their proper light before the community, compel me to do so, as it would be expected that he should by all means honorable endeavor to avenge his father's death.

Though known to be a man void of truth, yet, under the circumstances, he was enabled by the aid of the Charleston Courier to make an impression prejudicial to Monroe. Had the difficulty not originated between himself and Byrd Monroe, which originated out of some of said *gentleman's known veracity*, the evening before, and his reports of said difficulty to his father, Monroe and Ellington would yet be living, as Monroe was at the time making arrangement to remove his family from out of the influence of the said Monroe's family; and had James D. Ellington told the truth to his father, at night, Adolphus would not have been mixed up in the difficulty.

To describe the appearance of the mob on the fatal morning, would be impossible; but most men have seen some few men under the influence of passion, and of the worst; when we add to this the deleterious effects of alcohol on some four or five thousand we may behold the mob.

We will give the public a few of those who were most active in urging on and collecting the mob.

Jas. Cunningham,	Jefferson Coleman,
Jas. D. Ellington,	Allen Coleman,
Dennis Hanks,	John Eperson.
William Eperson,	

The Tools.

John Allen,	Thomas Bradford,
John Kelley,	John Jones,
J. B. Kelley,	Drew Wallace,
—— Vanvarus,	Robert Davis,
William Hart,	French of Saulsberry,
Henry Stephens,	Dr. Furguson,
David Fansler,	McNary of Clark Co.
Will Little,	Jackson White,
J. J. Conley,	Thomas Eperson,
Sol. Cossel,	Wm. Love,
Thomas Fleming,	Nap. Stone,
Samuel French,	Martin Runnels.
Jas. Eastin,	John Hunlsneer,
Samuel Gray,	Esq. Gard,
Wm. Hinchman,	Thos. Fleming, the hangman.

We could go on and give you divers other names, some of whom we do not know, but these few may answer. N. B. Aulick.

Falmouth, Kentucky, *December* 21, 1856.

The undersigned are now and have been citizens severally, of the county of Pendleton, State of Kentucky, for near forty years; much the greater portion of which period, they have resided in the town of Falmouth, the seat of justice of the county. Adolphus F. Monroe, who was barbarously and brutally murdered by an infuriated mob in February, 1856, at Charleston, Coles county, State of Illinois, was well know by *them*, from his infancy up to his cruel and lawless death. He was born and raised in their said town (one of them was his guardian during his minority), and his family and kindred are well and intimately known to them, as neighbors, fellow-townsmen and citizens. Both his parents were, and are members of families of as high repute, merit, and respectability, as the most vain could desire to boast of. His mother is the daughter of David Clarkson, Esq., now deceased, an early settler in this section of the State; he lived to an advanced stage of life; died, leaving a numerous family, his descendants, many years since, respected, beloved, and regretted by all whose favor it was to have made his acquaintance while living.

The father of Adolphus was Jeremiah Monroe, an early citizen of the village. He was a physician of distinction, by profession; commenced an extensive practice, and was noted for his benevolence, as a practitioner and man; for his many virtues, his moral worth, sterling and unbending integrity and candor as a citizen, as well as an exemplary deportment as a professor and Christian, and as a kind and devoted father. Dr. Monroe departed this life in the year 1831; and now lies buried within one-and-a-half miles of Falmouth, the place in which he had practiced his profession for many years anterior to his death, and near which he died sincerely bemoaned and lamented by all who knew him.

At the time of the death of Dr. Jeremiah Monroe, he left surviving him, his afflicted and bereft wife and three infant children—an only son and two daughters. That only son was Adolphus F. Monroe, then only about four years old, and who, with a senior and a junior sister, composed the family, the care and moral nurture whereof devolved upon the widowed mother, as head and protector, with means, as to comforts of worldly effects, limited in extent. For, though the father was a good physician, commanding, in his day, a large practice, yet it was his fate, not to have accumulated a large estate. Upon the mother, Mrs. Maria Monroe, his widow, principally, was cast the effort to maintain, rear and educate her infant children. No orphans, perhaps, were ever blessed with a more affectionate and devoted mother, or who, for kindness and benevolence of heart, not only toward her own children, but wherever sickness and distress demanded relief, commanded to a greater extent, the regard and the respect of her neighbors and acquaintances. Though of a delicate physical constitution, and of feeble corporeal powers, none performed more faithfully all the duties of mother and neighbor; and none perhaps, succeeded better, in rearing her little family flock, or was more deeply imbued with an abiding sense of christian morality and the precepts of integrity and honor; and none deserved less the inhuman and barbarous fate, cruelly inflicted upon a widowed mother's heart, than the Charleston mob, with all its hellish and inhuman monstrosities, inflicted upon her, a stranger and homeless woman in their midst, in the savage, the barbarous and the lawless murder and death of her only son,—be he guilty or innocent of the offense charged against him.

The undersigned have known that son, Adolphus F. Monroe, from his cradle to his manhood, and thereafter up to 1852, then aged about twenty-five years, when he left his native village or town for Charleston, Coles county, Illinois. His standing and character as a boy—his standing and character as a man, while in the county and town of his birth—was that of respectability, that of morality, sobriety and good deportment, as well as honesty and integrity. No youth raised, within the memory of the undersigned, in the town or county of his birth, commanded more the regard and respect of his fellow-citizens, for a high sense of honor, moral deportment, and due observance of all the proprieties and courtesies and decencies of life—none, more devotedly attached or subservient in all his efforts, to relieve the wants of a widowed mother and her orphan children. He received, by the efforts of that mother, and of his own and that of friends, a substantial common English education, at the Pendleton Academy in this place; possessed more than an ordinary active, apt and intelligent mind, and no youth, according to the circumstances which surrounded him, had brighter and more promising prospects in the future; and though of an ardent and rather impulsive temperament, especially where his honor or integrity was in the remotest manner casually or intentionally involved, yet none were more true or sincere in friendship or family affections; none more willing or faithful in consecrating his earliest efforts and labors to the aid of a widowed mother and her family. And if ever there was aught whispered to his disparagement, or an accusation of crime or offense against him, before he left Kentucky in 1852, for Charleston, Ill., or prior to the charge against him in 1856, of having unfortunately, in an affray, killed his father-in-law, it is wholly unknown to the undersigned, who had full and open opportunity and every reasonable facility to know his every-day walk from his birth until 1852.

Judicial murders, or lawless mob murders, perpetrated within a country like ours, which boasts of its liberty, and as being regulated by laws absolutely protective of the life, property and characters of its individual citizens, are, upon the supposition that such atrocities have but too frequently transpired, mournful and inauspicious subjects, presented to the serious contemplation of the lover of his country and its republican form of government; if not positively ominous against the experiment now in progress of testing itself, upon this Continent; whether any people are sufficiently intelligent and virtuous and law-abiding in themselves, to govern themselves, and while so doing to confer reliable security and safety upon individuals, in the enjoyment of private property, life, and civil liberty. Be the signs of the times what they may,—and the action of mobs against life and upon court-houses, as temples dispensing law and justice, where life and property are in jeopardy—either auspicious or inauspicious as to the perpetuity or destruction of the government, the 15th of February, 1856, will ever mournfully be borne in memory in the simple annals of the town of Falmouth, as the day upon which the inhumanly beaten and cruelly mangled dead body of Adolphus F. Monroe arrived in town, accompanied and guarded by his heart-stricken and grief-distracted mother, wife, sister, and brother-in-law, having been forced to flee with that body from the worse than savage and lawless mob of Charleston and seek protection and refuge in his native town, and a grave for one of its native sons. The respect and sympathy entertained for him, as one of its native sons, and of those who knew him from his childhood, and his family, were mournfully manifested upon the day following, by a solemn funeral procession, larger than is usually congregated upon ordinary occasions, following his mangled corpse to the little island, in the bosom of one of our rivers, selected by himself while the mob was being collected to take his life, as the romantic spot endeared by happy reminiscences of past days; and to which he requested his mortal remains to be consigned. And there he now reposes, with the clods which weigh heavily upon his bosom consecrated by the bitter tears of a mother, an only sister and his wife, all present upon the last sad, solemn occasion; and that wife affectionately devoted to him in death, the daughter of him whom, it is alleged, he deprived of life with a murderous intent; while no one who knew him as a boy and as a man, in the long list of acquaintances and associates of his earlier days, is willing to believe that Adolphus F. Monroe ever committed homicide with *malice prepense* at heart.

S. Thos. Hauser.
Reuben McCarty.
James Wilson.

APPENDIX.

THE MONROE CASE.

HOW IT WAS CONDUCTED—GEN. LINDER'S CONDUCT.

CHARLESTON, *March 29th*, 1856.

MR. NAPOLEON B. AULICK:

Dear Sir:—Many things have been said, public and private, of my defense of your brother-in-law, A. F. Monroe. It has been charged that I did not defend him with my usual zeal and ability. Now, sir, I wish you to state your opinion frankly and freely upon this subject; for, whether it is against me or for me, I intend to give it to the public.

Yours, truly,

U. F. LINDER.

CHARLESTON, *Ill.*, *April 23d*, 1856.

MR. USHER F. LINDER:

Dear Sir:—Yours of the 29th ult. should have met with earlier attention at my hands, but, supposing that you wished my free and unreserved opinion, and also presuming that if the *facts* upon which that opinion is based, accompanied the opinion, it would prove not only very acceptable to you, but serve, at the same time, as a complete vindication of your course as the counsel of my late unfortunate brother-in-law, A. F. Monroe.

You will doubtless remember, that on the day upon which my brother-in-law was unfortunate enough to take the life of Mr. Nathan Ellington, his father-in-law, in an affray between them, you was employed to defend Monroe, charging only the *moderate* and *reasonable* fee of $1,000 for your services. You took charge of the case, and for some reason or other, the nature of which I do not know, refused to allow your client to appear before the examining court. However, it may be well enough for me to state (in order that the public may be made fully acquainted with the *fairness* and *zeal for the cause of your client*, and the *honorable* manner in which you commenced, and continued to the end, the conducting of the case), that on the day Ellington was shot, and in a few minutes after you was employed, you started out to collect the evidence for the defense. On your hunt after evidence, you met A. G. Jones, Esq., one of the lawyers for the prosecution, and *told him that you had started out with the intention of going round the public square, but had not got more than half around, and had found, in that small compass, not only evidence enough to hang your present client, but, you was afraid to go the remainder of the circuit, for fear you should find evidence enough to "lap over" and hang some of your future clients!* Now, sir, who can doubt that you conducted the case with your "usual zeal and ability," when you *commenced* by telling the above to one of the prosecuting attorneys? I can not, have not, and do not doubt it? Well, a few days after the above acknowledgment to Mr Jones, and while Ellington was *yet alive,* the preliminary examination of Monroe was held. At that examination you not only would not permit your client to be present, but actually refused to introduce witnesses in his behalf, witnesses whose testimony would have been favorable to his cause; and allowed the prosecution to introduce and examine theirs; *literally making no defense,* and pledging yourself that your client *should not* have a change of venue, and stating that you was *authorized by your client* to make such statement, and that it was his (your client's) determination to stand his trial at the next term of the court. That statement, sir, was false. Your client *did not* authorize you to make any such pledge, and you not only knew it, but, also, you knew it was his intention to have made application for a change of venue, as he, and every one else, was fully aware of the impossibility of his obtaining a fair and impartial trial in this county. I was absent from town the day of the preliminary examination, and was not aware of your pledging your client for a trial in this county, until the Saturday before the term of the court, called for the trial of this case, in February last, when I happened to see a notice to that effect in the "Courier" which was issued the week preceding the trial. I immediately came to you with the paper containing that announcement, and asked you if such was the fact, and if you had made such a pledge. Your reply was that you had. I then asked you if you intended to redeem that pledge. You replied that you *must* do it—was *compelled* to redeem it, from the fact that this was your home; that all your property was here, and here was your all; with home, property, reputation, your all at stake, you could not do *otherwise* than redeem that pledge; and that your *only regret was,* that you had not told Monroe and myself of the existence of that pledge sooner, so that I might have employed other counsel in the case. Then, sir, I informed you that you could consider yourself no longer a counsel in the case; that *I* would not submit to my friend and brother being tried in any such manner. You then agreed to leave the case. James Monroe and I then went down to your office, and I took up my note, and the mortgage on my land, which I had given you to secure your fee. This was on the Saturday night previous to the sitting of the court, which commenced on the Monday following. You said you released every thing in relation to the fee, thanking your God for making you *too honest* to exact a fee under such circumstances, stating that you would just as soon *steal* the money as to exact it for attempting his defense here ; that Monroe *might just as well be taken out into the street and shot, as to be tried in Coles county.* You then *dictated*, while James Monroe wrote an application to the judge for a change of venue, which *I* was to hand to the prisoner, and *he* to Judge Harlan. You then *volunteered* your services to James Monroe and myself, *to put off the trial* (as you considered *that* a much safer plan for the prisoner than to apply for the change of venue, as the *mob* had determined there should be no change), on the grounds that the prisoner was not prepared to enter upon his trial, important witnesses for the defense being absent. You also stated that if you could *not* get a continuation of the trial on *that ground*, you *would* do so by *challenging* the jurors.

Perfectly relying upon your *promises*, and having the utmost confidence in your *integrity* and *honesty* in the matter, I left the case to be managed by you, in your own way; fully understanding that if you did not succeed in putting off the trial, then *we* were to make the application for a change of venue.

On Monday evening the grand jury reported a true bill against the prisoner, and on Tuesday morning, when I entered the court-room, I was not only astonished to find that you had made no effort to have the trial continued, but that part of the jury was already impanneled, and the remainder were being found among the crowd, and you did not challenge one of them ! As I do not wish to lose one item that may prove beneficial to you in setting your conduct right before the people, I will now state what I should have done before a remark you made during the conversation with James Monroe and myself, held at your office on the Saturday night preceding the trial. You said, that if we succeeded in getting the change of venue, and got the prisoner out of the county, and wished you to do so, you would *then* appear for and *clear him in spite of h—ll!* and that the *most* that could be made against him would be *manslaughter*.

After you had gone into the trial, you drew up a note for $910, (having received, previously, $90 out of the $1,000), took it to the jail, after night, and got the prisoner to sign it, securing said note by a mortgage on 160 acres of land belonging to the prisoner.

And, again, on Tuesday morning of the term, before you entered into the trial, you turned to the mass in the court-room, whom you conceived to be the *mob*, and asked of *them* if *they* would allow *you* the *privilege* of defending the *prisoner !*

The trial consumed the entire week, and as everybody knew it would be so, the jury, as a *matter of course*, returned a verdict of "Guilty of Murder in the First Degree" against the prisoner. When the jury came down to give in their verdict, you were absent, and the judge refused to receive it until you were *present, by your client,* and you were sent for, but *refused* to come, and the prisoner received it *alone!* On Monday morning Judge Harlan called the court together, for the purpose of passing sentence on Monroe. You then appeared in court before the sentence was passed, and made a motion for a new trial, founding your motion upon some plan in the instructions to the jury. The judge took until Tuesday morning to consider the motion, examine authorities, etc. During that same day you came to me and told me that, *in order to save Monroe's life from the mob,* you thought it was best for you to go to the judge and get him to overrule the motion, and allow him to pass sentence upon the prisoner, and you would take the instructions to the Supreme Court, and get a new trial from that body. Tuesday morning came, the motion was overruled, and sentence was passed upon Monroe. *Then you refused to go to the Supreme Court, saying that your duties in the case had ceased! It was several days before I could induce you to go up to the Supreme Court, as you had said you designed doing when you wanted your motion overruled by Judge Harlan.* Previously to your taking the papers up to Springfield, you stated publicly, in Bill Hart's grocery, that you were *going* up to the Supreme Court, *not for the purpose of getting a new trial, but, seemingly to discharge your duty and for the satisfaction of his (Monroe's) friends!*

After you got to Springfield, you stated that *you did not want a new trial,* and when the application for the new trial was decided against you in that court, you said *it was decided just as you wanted it!*

Now, sir, you have your whole conduct as counsel for A. F. Monroe, above. I have told it truly, calmly, and fairly. Now you shall have my opinion. So far from your conducting the case with zeal and ability of *any kind*, saying nothing about the "usual," I believe you were either most woefully indifferent to the fate of your client, lamentably deficient in honesty, or feed to hang Dolph Monroe by the mob—the other side. You can choose either horn of the dilemma you please—it was *one* of the *three,* and, most likely the latter, as you said, after the failure of your application to the Supreme Court, that you *wished the mob would hang him!* Is it not astonishing, sir, this depravity of human nature? You were right in thanking your God that he made you *so honest;* and I do not blame you, for no one else can do the same for you. No, Mr. Linder, your conduct in the case was this: it was cowardly, it was dishonorable, it was dishonest, it was two-faced. You would profess one thing and act another. But, sir, I have done. I hope you are fully satisfied with my "thoughts upon this subject," and with that hope, allow me, sir, to subscribe myself,

Respectfully, your obedient servant,

NAPOLEON B. AULICK.

CHARLESTON, *January 30th*, 1856.

N. B. AULICK :—

Dear, Dear Friend :—When I am gone, take my Diaries, Books No. 1 and 2, to Emmerson Bennett of Cincinnati, or some other man competent to write out and expose all of this affair ; and my last solemn request is, that *no name—no man or woman be spared :*—let the truth be told, and even the very names given as they are. This I solemnly request.

Pole, you are the only *man I ever loved,* and I have loved you far beyond a *brother's love*—I would have *died* for you ; for *you have* a heart—you are a *man*—and *an honest man,* and they are very scarce in this world. I have tried to be your *friend*—I am now going to God—and to you and my mother I leave ALL I HAVE. All I request of you is, do for me, when I am gone, as you *think I would do for you.* You know what I mean, *for you have a heart*—you are a man. Pole, do not grieve for me, when I am gone. I'm *ready*—I am going home. We 'll meet again—*up there*—up there we 'll meet and *rejoice.* Comfort my poor old mother—*'t will not be long.* I go prepared. I only *ask* of you, see these books published—see it done. My name shall yet be mighty and strong ; my name and memory shall yet be all powerful for *vengeance,* when I am dust. My life and my words shall yet be a common and familiar sound in every household in the land—and I will yet be most *terribly avenged*—and my name endeared to all *honest men and women.*

Pole, when I am gone take me to *Kentucky*—take me from here, bury me upon *Kentucky* soil—upon one of the islands above Falmouth, "St. Helena," or Lover's Retreat. Inclose *it,* etc., as you will find directed in my books—a weeping willow at my head, and a cedar at my feet—future generations shall visit my tomb and shed tears upon my grave.

Nannie has done this thing; but her mother led her on. Spare her, for my child's sake ; spare her, when I am gone. She must and will suffer much—add not to the stings of her own conscience.

That is surely enough. But should she ever marry again, then I invoke all the curses of hell and heaven upon her head.

Pole, if I was free but one day, I would not fall alone, or *unavenged.* God restrains my arm.—He will yet avenge my fall and fate. When I am moldering in my grave, I will still *speak* and be avenged.

Nannie has loved me well ; alas ! too well, for she has been ever jealous ; and I had rather, to-day, be in my place and go to eternity, than in hers, with her conscience, and live ; and I prophesy right here, that she will not stay long. Her heart, I think, is right—and she and her relatives can never get along. *She can never be happy again.*

Pole, when I am gone, I want you and my mother to save all you can of my estate, from *Linder* the thief, and from the hands of the law, for your own use. Attend to my requests, *all* of them, and one is; save what you can for you and my mother.

Keep an eye upon my child, while she lives; I don't think she will ever live to be a woman; and I prefer that she would die than to be raised there. Oh God! let her not stay there. Nannie has sworn to me that *she* herself, nor May, should stay there.

Pole, I have loved Nannie and *spoiled* her. She was a *spoiled child,* and I petted and spoiled her as my wife. I had to *conquer all this—and I have done so.* She was *completely conquered* and a *good and loving wife* when this affair occurred. She was a *child,* but she is now a *woman.* She was, when this thing happened, a *good wife* and a *true woman;* 'tis true, she has caused all; but blame her mother, and not her. *Her mother has murdered* Ellington and me, and how many more God alone may know. If Nannie redeems half of her promises and pledges to me, when I am gone, *she is worthy*—if not, she *must and will suffer.*

Pole—dear, dear, noble friend, this earth is but a stopping-place. You and I, Pole, will meet again and then you may know how well I love you. *I am no common man;* I am above—far above—the vulgar *herd,* and so are you, in HEART, if not in education.

In another and better world, Pole, we'll meet again, my noble friend, the ONLY MAN I ever *loved.*

I have done—I fall—but remember I fall a victim, *but proudly fall!* In eternity, all this thing shall be solved. A man can die but once, and he who fears to die, is *not a man.* This day I would only ask *life*—only ask to live for those *I love,* and for my own *fame. I am a man;* my *spirit, before God, will tower far* above the low, dirty world. Pole! I am *prepared*—I am safe—meet *me there;* meet me there, my noble-hearted friend and brother. *God is our Judge,* and we will conquer and rejoice with Him. Weep not for me, I am at rest! *I have gone home!*

A. F. MONROE.

THE END.

www.ingramcontent.com/pod-product-compliance
Lightning Source LLC
LaVergne TN
LVHW021426110826
845150LV00007B/2098
* 9 7 8 1 4 2 5 5 0 8 5 8 6 *